KENNETH S. HEMPHILL

Spiritual Gifts

EMPOWERING the NEW TESTAMENT CHURCH

BROADMAN PRESS
Nashville, Tennessee

Unless otherwise stated, all Scripture quotations are from the
New American Standard Bible. Copyright © The Lockman
Foundation, 1960, 1962, 1963, 1968, 1971, 1972, 1973, 1975,
1977. Used by permission. Scripture quotations marked KJV are
from the King James Version of the Bible.
Scripture quotations marked NEB are from *The New English
Bible*. Copyright © The Delegates of the Oxford University
Press and the Syndics of the Cambridge University Press, 1961,
1970. Reprinted by permission.
Scripture quotations marked Moffatt are from *The Bible: a New
Translation* by James A. R. Moffatt. Copyright © 1935 by Harp-
er and Row, Publishers, Inc. Used by permission.

Library of Congress Cataloging-in-Publication Data

Hemphill, Kenneth S., 1948–
    Spiritual gifts : empowering the New Testament church / Kenneth
S. Hemphill.
        p.   cm.
    ISBN 0-8054-5918-9 : $5.95
    1. Gifts, Spiritual—History of doctrines—Early church, ca.
30-600.   2. Bible.   N.T.   Epistles of Paul—Criticism, interpretation, etc.   I. Title.
BT767.3.H45 1988
234'.13'09015—dc19   88-6913
                                                          CIP

To the special people who inspired,
encouraged, and supported my original
study on which this book is based:
—C. F. D. Moule, former Lady Margaret
Professor at Cambridge University;
—Carl and Ruby Hemphill, my parents;
—Paul and Daphne Moore, my parents-in-law;
—and Paula, my wife, without whose
love and support this work would not
have been possible.

Preface

A Small Step In God's Plan

The repetitious and driving sound of drums, organ, tambourine, and guitar penetrated the stillness of the small North Carolina town of my childhood. The volume of the noise seemed grossly out of proportion to the small tent erected behind the corner grocery store near my home. From the safety of the rolled-down window of my dad's '57 Pontiac, I watched in wide-eyed wonder as the revival service got into full swing. "Scary" and "strange" were the best terms that my twelve-year-old vocabulary could muster to describe the proceedings of that evening. Such was my first, but certainly not my last encounter with Pentecostal religion.

I found it easy to dismiss my first exposure to Pentecostalism's religious fervor as nothing more than a curious novelty. It was not to be taken seriously. It would pass like all religious fads. But I soon learned that I was wrong to group all Pentecostals in one basket and treat them as objects of my "more-informed-than-you" pity. The Lord often seems to display a sense of humor when He desires to teach us helpful lessons in humility. You could have knocked me over with a feather when I discovered that my best friend in junior high was the son of a Pentecostal pastor. To my amazement my friend was perfectly normal and so was his father. We didn't discuss theology very often, but we did enjoy a close friendship. Occasionally we visited one another's churches. While I still preferred our style of worship, some of the stigma had been removed from my childhood impression by this personal encounter.

I had learned that it was unfair and inaccurate to pigeonhole all "Pentecostals" and stereotype them as persons who had immaturely given in to emotionalism. All of us have found it increasingly difficult to dismiss charismatics or Pentecostals. Many people have friends or perhaps family members who worship in a charismatic church. They testify to a deeper level of commitment. Frequently we have witnessed a change in their behavior. Occasionally we have wondered if they have something we've been missing. On the other hand, Pentecostals are increasingly seeking some biblical roots for what they believe to be a valid and meaningful experience.

The phenomenal growth of the Pentecostal and charismatic movements have created intriguing and sometimes awkward questions for pastors and laypersons alike. Do the spiritual gifts still exist? Are all the gifts still active? If not, why did some pass away? How many gifts are there? Do I have any? Is it OK to pray for certain gifts? Do I need to speak in tongues to be baptized with the Holy Spirit? Why doesn't our church permit tongues? Am I missing something vital? Perhaps it is best summed up in the question, "Pastor, what do we believe about the spiritual gifts?"

Seminary provided a suitable environment to further my search for understanding of a complex issue. The Pentecostal movement had not gone away as many pastors had predicted. It had in fact grown in scope and visibility. Some of the major Pentecostal churches were a far cry from the small tent behind the corner grocery or the clapboard building on the back streets of my hometown. Now I was faced with large growing Pentecostal churches and well-known figures who testified to a charismatic experience. I still needed answers for some unresolved and demanding questions.

I wouldn't want to give you the impression that this was the only issue on my mind during my seminary years. In truth, as I look back on that pilgrimage, I can't even say it was the most pressing question. Yet it was an issue that for me, and others like me, cried for a clear word.

How then was I thrust upon a course of study that would eventually lead to a graduate-level thesis on spiritual gifts? A reasonable question. As graduation from seminary approached I began to struggle with issues, at that time, more pressing than spiritual gifts. Issues like a job, a family, and earning a living. I had relatives who had already expressed the concern that I had been called to be a professional student.

As God's plan began to unfold, my wife and I felt a clear leading that the Lord was directing us to further graduate studies. It was to be in a most unlikely setting—Cambridge, England. The application and acceptance procedure stretched into months as the correspondence was a slow process. During this time I knew I had to decide on a topic for research. I needed a field of study that I could live with for the three years of required residence. Of one thing I was sure! I had committed my life to the pastoral ministry and I wanted to concentrate my New Testament studies in a field that would prepare me to be a more effective pastor. From my own experience, I knew that this question of spiritual gifts was one that I must answer for my own satisfaction as well as for the good of my church family. I could not afford to be uninformed, nor could I afford to miss out on the full empowering of God for the church. It was certainly no accident that God brought me back to those unresolved questions of childhood. Through much prayer and wise counsel, I decided upon graduate study concentrating on the nature and purpose of spiritual gifts in the New Testament church. From a twelve-year-old, wide-eyed kid at a tent revival to an enrolling graduate student was really just a small step in God's sovereign plan.

Narrowing The Focus

All seemed to be in order until I arrived in Cambridge. I discovered rather quickly that I had chosen a large and complex topic. Would I interact with the growing number of "popular" books either encouraging or discouraging one to "experience" the gifts? Would I deal with similar estatic phenomena such as tongues outside the Christian faith? Should I focus narrowly on the function of gifts in the New

Testament communities? The latter option was my choice, and it is still my conviction that we must first come to terms with the evidence of the New Testament and then formulate our present-day practice to conform to the biblical pattern. Too often we are swayed in our thinking by "experiences" of "friends" or "success stories." The focus on the New Testament evidence will provide a stable platform to understand and evaluate current experiences.

Arriving At A Procedure

For months in England I struggled to get a handle on the New Testament material. My study convinced me that there were differences in emphasis and content in the various passages where Paul dealt with "spiritual gifts." In some passages the language concerning spiritual gifts is lacking, but the content about community ministry is clearly present. Some letters contain no mention of community ministry at all. The discussion of the more "miraculous gifts" such as tongues, healing, and miracle-working faith seems to be limited to 1 Corinthians. How do we understand the differences from letter to letter if the spiritual gifts were the empowering force of the New Testament church? Now at this point you might be wondering which passages in the Pauline letters are relevant to the study of spiritual gifts. After much consideration, I chose to limit this study to the four major passages in which Paul addressed the matter of the ongoing ministry of the local church.

The passages we will be looking at in some detail are 1 Thessalonians 5:12-22, 1 Corinthians 12—14, Romans 12, and Ephesians 4:1-16. The first and last passages provide us with a historical picture frame around the extensive treatment of spiritual gifts in 1 Corinthians 12—14. A quick glance at these passages will alert you to the fact that neither 1 Thessalonians nor Ephesians contain a specific reference to "spiritual gifts." Yet these passages are equally important to our study, and the omission of the term "spiritual gifts" is itself significant.

Most of us, if asked about spiritual gifts, would turn immediately to 1 Corinthians 12—14. There can be little doubt that we must give great attention to this passage if we are to formulate a clear understanding of the role of spiritual gifts in the New Testament church. But it would be a great mistake to consider this text without due attention to the passages, similar in content, which both precede and follow it. Many of the treatments of this topic go astray by neglecting the other community ministry passages. Further, it would be wrong to attempt to interpret any of these texts without first reconstructing the historical situation that prompted the writing and shaped the particular emphasis of that letter.

The procedure of this study will therefore be obvious and straightforward. I will examine each of the previously mentioned passages in its chronological order[1]. The first concern will be to develop a clear picture of the historical situation and to give suggestions as to why a passage concerning community ministry has been included in that particular letter. Only after the examination of the historical and contextual situation, will I begin to comment on such matters as the nature and purpose of spiritual gifts.

Here are a few words of caution. One could overemphasize the impact of the historical situation on the content of a given letter. This could give the impression that Paul was an opportunist and that he altered his teaching to fit the need of the moment. Truly that would be a distorted portrait of Paul. Yet to ignore the truth that Paul's teaching came to written formulation in response to *unique* and *real* historical situations is to overlook a key for understanding Pauline thought. We cannot fail to take into account Paul's pastoral ability to emphasize certain elements of his teaching in order to meet the needs of a particular community.

Many mistakes in judgement have been made by not taking into account the total picture. Buying a dress or suit on credit and not taking into account the interest that will accrue or running through a caution light at an intersection without due attention to the oncoming traffic are everyday examples of not seeing the total picture. The Scripture, taken in the same type of disjointed manner, can lead to confusion and misinterpretation.

A study which causes us to examine both the mind and experience of Paul and the historical and pastoral context of each passage should lead us to a deeper appreciation of the miracle of inspiration. Paul was moved by the Spirit of God to write letters to address unique pastoral problems in specific historical communities, yet they speak with power and clarity to Christians today.

This is a study that flows from the Bible. The reader will find it essential to read this book with an open Bible. I believe that by a careful study of the empowering of the New Testament church we will find answers to our personal questions about spiritual gifts. But beyond that it is my desire that we rediscover the dynamic and empowering of the church that "turned the world upside down" (Acts 17:6, KJV).

Note

1. The date of writing of the Pauline letters is a complex issue. Most Bible scholars agree with the order that I consider these four passages.

Contents

Final

Ewert

Ch. 5, 6, 12

Foreword

Dr. Kenneth Hemphill is an arresting example of the giftedness about which he writes with such clarity. A varsity football player at Wake Forrest, he later distinguished himself as a student at Southern Baptist Theological Seminary. Then he earned the Ph.D. in New Testament at Cambridge University. After returning from England he entered the pastorate. As pastor of First Baptist Church, Norfolk, Virginia, since 1981, God has used him in a ministry that has captured the interest of the entire East Coast as well as the Tidewater area. The church has grown from an average Sunday School attendance in the three-hundreds to more than two thousand in a six-year period. As a guest preacher, I experienced personally the gifted vitality of this exploding congregation. Dr. Hemphill is qualified both personally and pastorally to write about spiritual gifts in the New Testament.

He has authored a book that the times demand. Existing popular literature on spiritual gifts largely attempts to define each gift. Dr. Hemphill provides a study that is first historical and contextual. He informs us that Paul's teaching about spiritual gifts was in response to unique and real historical situations. Using careful scholarship presented in a popular style, he details the varying church situations which produced 1 Thessalonians 5, 1 Corinthians 12—14, Romans 12, and Ephesians 4. He traces the natural progression in Paul's thought that was called out by the differing church situations. He makes a compelling case that spiritual gifts must not be isolated from the concrete Christian communities addressed by Paul. Dr. Hemphill

15

avoids the practice of lifting the spiritual gift passages out of context and using them to defend or attack practices in today's churches.

The author demonstrates that 1 Thessalonians 5 is a seminal passage for Paul's later teaching. Paul emphasized to that church the unique role of the ministering community. Each member is accountable for ministry in the church. Although spiritual gifts are not discussed as such in 1 Thessalonians, Dr. Hemphill finds the germinal thought that led to the expanded discussion in 1 Corinthians 12—14.

The author's profound historical, contextual, and exegetical grasp is most clearly demonstrated in his full analysis of the Corinthian passage. While he continues his study of the gifts in the ancient Corinthian church, he draws provocative parallels between its situation and contemporary charismatic debate. He demonstrates the striking similarity between the "overrealized eschatology" at Corinth and the contemporary American "health-and-wealth gospel." The Corinthian church arrogance that felt free to live above accepted moral behavior finds striking parallels in the recent headlines of our newspapers. The sometimes arrogance and exclusiveness of contemporary charismatics had its clear counterparts at Corinth. Dr. Hemphill cogently presents the evidence that gifts alone do not make a person more spiritual than others.

The Norfolk pastor presents 1 Corinthians 13 as a vital part of the gifts discussion, not as a parenthesis. Unlike those who see the passage as a "love poem" imported from Paul's other preaching or writing, the author sees it as a necessary corrective for the Corinthians' aberrant understanding of gifts. 1 Corinthians 13 is Paul's "redefinition of the spiritual person." For the pulpiteer, this discussion alone would merit this book. Dr. Hemphill continues his emphasis on "gifts in community" in his treatment of 1 Corinthians 14. Here Paul brings the spiritual gifts "back to earth" by emphasizing their role in the common good of the community. In short, if a gift does not edify, it does not help.

In contrast to the polemical nature of 1 Corinthians, the Romans 12 passage is more "neutral." The author makes it abundantly clear that Paul wanted to exalt those gifts that most led to the edification of the body. The unique emphasis in Ephesians relates to Paul's desire to protect the Asian church from heretical teachings. Here the emphasis rests on those leadership and teaching gifts which give the church doctrinal stability. Dr. Hemphill demonstrates again the relationship of spiritual gifts to definite Christian communities.

Dr. Hemphill insists that gifts cannot be separated from ethics and that the gifts of the Spirit cannot be separated from the fruit of the Spirit. That is, what a person *is* cannot ultimately be separated from what a person *does*. Spiritual gifts can be sought, controlled, and developed, but they cannot be separated from what a person is.

Most of us in the preaching ministry have a collection of books on the charismatic question and the spiritual gifts. These books come from several viewpoints. Some defend contemporary charismatic conduct. Others reject categorically modern use of spiritual gifts. Still others are mere definitions of the words Paul used to describe each gift. I do not know of a book in the same category as this work by the winsome young pastor at Norfolk. He brings a technical scholar's skills, a popular pastor's heart, and a contemporary communicator's ability to this debated question. We will all profit for years from this treatment. This book is a gift from a gifted fellow servant.

Joel C. Gregory
Travis Avenue Baptist Church
Fort Worth, Texas

1
An Early Look at Ministry Structure

"Elementary, my dear Watson . . ." You no doubt recognize that familiar quote from the master detective Sherlock Holmes. Sherlock could always put together bits and pieces of information to baffle the reader and most assuredly Mr. Watson with his ability to formulate a hypothesis.

Gathering Clues at Thessalonica

First and 2 Thessalonians, taken together with the narrative in Acts 17:1-10, provide us with a limited amount of material with which to produce a detailed picture of the situation in Thessalonica. To put the puzzle together we must ask some difficult questions. How long was Paul in Thessalonica? Did he establish an ongoing community with pastoral leadership? If so, did he leave any instructions for ministry? Is there a reference to spiritual gifts?

The consideration of this passage is important for our study for several reasons. It is acknowledged to be one of Paul's earliest letters and it contains a significant passage which addresses the concerns of the ongoing ministry of a local community.

"Elementary, you say." Well, let's see if we can unravel the mystery of the historical situation which prompted this letter. We will gather clues from 1 and 2 Thessalonians and Acts.

According to Acts, Paul began his ministry in Thessalonica by reasoning in the synagogue for *three Sabbaths*. The scene then abruptly shifted to the uproar that resulted in the harassment of Jason and the brethren and the quick departure of Paul. While the evidence is

18

admittedly slight, there are several indicators from the letters which, when taken together, suggest that Paul's ministry in Thessalonica was considerably longer than the three sabbaths mentioned in Acts.

A few clues:

1. Paul was in Thessalonica long enough to set up his own trade (1 Thess. 2:9).

2. An intimate loving relationship such as the letter clearly alludes to could scarcely have developed in a few weeks (1 Thess. 2:7-12, 17, 19; 3:6).

3. If Paul ministered only a few weeks in Thessalonica, could the church have grown sufficiently strong to have become a model to all believers in Macedonia and Achaia (1 Thess. 1:8-9)?

4. The presence of organized leadership, however elementary, suggests a period longer than three weeks.

5. Apparently Paul was in Thessalonica sufficiently long to receive aid twice from the Philippians (Phil. 4:16).

If we suggest that Paul remained in Thessalonica for a period considerably longer than three weeks, a second question emerges. What was the location of his ministry following the expulsion from the synagogue? Neither Thessalonians nor Acts tell us directly, but there are several important clues.

If we look at Paul's pattern for ministry in other communities we can gain some insight into the likely sequence of events in Thessalonica. In Corinth, Paul began his ministry by reasoning in the synagogue every Sabbath. As resistance arose among the Jews, he left the synagogue and continued his ministry in the home of Titus Justus (Acts 18:4-7). The flow of events was similar at Ephesus. Paul entered the synagogue and spoke boldly for three months. Again opposition arose and Paul withdrew with his followers and continued to teach in the school of Tyrannus (Acts 19:8-9).

Concerning Thessalonica, however, there is no specific mention of a ministry subsequent to the synagogue ministry. We find only the abbreviated report of a mob aroused by the Jews going to the house of Jason to apprehend Paul (Acts 17:1-10). When they did not find Paul, they brought Jason and some of the brethren before the city authorities. They were accused of upsetting the world and teaching contrary to the decrees of Caesar. In the light of Paul's absence, "Jason and the others" were required to guarantee the good behavior of their guests. Paul and Silas were then sent away secretly to Berea where the jurisdiction of the magistrates of Thessalonica was not valid.

Could the violent reaction of the Jews be explained in terms of Paul's three sabbaths at the synagogue? Was it not more likely that the hostility grew as Paul's ministry in Thessalonica continued fruitfully for several months at Jason's home? How did the mob know that Paul could be found at Jason's home? Why were certain brethren assembled there when the mob arrived? These questions are best answered by the suggestion that Jason's home had become the center for Christian activity, and Jason himself had emerged as one the leaders in the Christian community in Thessalonica.

While it is unlikely that the Christian communities faced systematic persecution during the apostolic period, both 1 Thessalonians and Acts indicate that the Thessalonian Christians were encountering some type of affliction. According to 1 Thessalonians 1:6; 2:2, 14-16; 3:1-5, the situation was serious enough to cause Paul great concern. The tribulation was probably a general harassment, coming perhaps from relatives and former friends. It reflected the hostility of both Jew and Gentile alike to the success of the new religious sect. The persecution that led to Paul's departure continued even after he was gone. This, in a large measure, accounts for the hasty writing of 1 Thessalonians and for much of its content.

It appears then that one of the methods of harassment which developed after Paul's departure was the attempt to destroy the Christian community by discrediting Paul and his work in Thessalonica. If the extensive self-defense in 1 Thessalonians 1—3 is a valid indicator, this procedure had met with some measure of success. Paul expressed his anxiety not only for the welfare of the Thessalonian Christians but also for their attitude toward him (3:6). You might wonder: How could the attacks on Paul's character and work have met with success, when the Thessalonians would have been aware of the fallacy of the accusations? The one clue that provides the key for understanding this matter is Paul's hasty and secretive departure. I suggest that Jason and a few brethren, a small inner circle of dedicated persons with whom Paul had spent much time, had sent Paul away quickly and secretly to guarantee his safety. This meant that many persons in the community were not personally aware of the details of Paul's departure. Jason had defended Paul's actions, but there were other brethren who had found Paul's sudden disappearance in the face of persecution inexcusable and had turned against their founder. The majority, however, were simply unsettled by Paul's absence, the accusations being leveled against him, and the mounting persecution.

Try putting yourself in their shoes. How would you feel if the man in whom you had placed great confidence suddenly left the church during a very difficult period. Remember you are a relatively new Christian. Now add to your loss the fact that you are bearing the brunt of harassment that had been prompted by this man's ministry. I think you can see why Paul would have been anxious to know if the Thessalonians still loved him.

Does this reconstruction find support from the content of the letter? Notice first that Paul devoted much of the first three chapters to a defense of his tactics, behavior, message, and results while in Thessalonica. As early as 1 Thessalonians 1:5, there is a reference to the uprightness of Paul's behavior. Paul defended himself by pointing to the visible testimony of their faith (1:6 to 2:2). He assured them that his message did not spring from error, impurity, or deceit (2:3; see 2:10). He did not come with flattering speech to win glory and approval from people (2:4-6). He could not be accused of greed (2:5b). He had worked night and day to support himself (2:9). The accusations reflected in Paul's defense arose out of the continuing hostility toward the Christians in Thessalonica and were aimed at discrediting Paul's ministry.

It is obvious that Paul's sudden disappearance and his failure to return (2:17-20) had provided his detractors with a golden opportunity to attack the young Christian community. The device of discrediting the teachings of a prominent man by casting doubt on his motives and conduct was frequently practiced in the time of the early church. Unfortunately there were enough frauds and wandering speakers of questionable motive, to make the method successful. Paul felt it necessary to defend his actions for the sake of the Thessalonians.

This method of discrediting a teacher or preacher by personal attack upon his or her character and motive did not cease with the New Testament era. All too often we encounter people in churches or denominations who attempt to discredit someone by unfounded attacks upon his character. Tragically, the innuendo itself is often enough to ruin. The other side of the coin has not changed that much either. There are frauds and charlatans today whose behavior casts doubt upon the integrity of all ministers.

Second, this letter abounds with references to Paul's affection for the Thessalonians and reminders of the relationship that had been established between the community and himself. Paul praised their witness in glowing terms (1:6-10). Verse 8 of 1 Thessalonians chapter 2 begins and ends with mention of Paul's love for them. In 3:12 a reference to Paul's affection for them literally intrudes itself into a doxology. When Paul received the good news from Timothy that the Thesalonians were standing firm in their love for Paul, he declared "now we really live" (3:8).

Third, the discussion of persecution and suffering has an apologetic undercurrent. Paul reminded them that he too had suffered at Philippi before coming to Thessalonica and that his ministry in Thessalonica was accomplished in the face of much opposition (2:2). Paul assured them that his departure and continued absence were not his choice (2:14-18). Paul compared their situation with that of the churches of Judea, demonstrating that all Christians must suffer (see 3:3 and the more explicit statement in 2 Thess. 1:4-5). Paul was careful to remind them that they were suffering persecution even before he left (2 Thess. 1:6), and he had warned them concerning affliction (2 Thess. 3:3-4). Simply put, he wanted them to realize that he had not been the cause of their persecution, nor were they the only Christians suffering.

The historical reconstruction offered here does explain the extended apology of chapters 1—3, the repeated emphasis on the loving relationship between the apostle and this community, and the apologetic undercurrent present in the discussion of suffering. How then does this reconstruction aid us in understanding the writing of the letter and the content of the passage we are considering?

Soon after his escape from Thessalonica, Paul's concern for the ongoing life of the young church prompted him to send Timothy to strengthen and encourage the believers (3:2). Timothy returned with a report that was, by and large, positive but with the news that there was some tension. It is further likely that Timothy informed Paul concerning other community problems and matters of misunderstanding.

Therefore Paul wrote this letter for several apparent reasons. He felt it necessary to vindicate himself fully for the sake of the community. His concern was not for his reputation but for the possible ill effects if the charges were left unanswered. Second, Paul wanted to assure their continued growth as a Christian community by building up their faith (3:10). Since circumstances had made it impossible to do this in person, he utilized this letter to remind them of several areas of his teaching and to add further elaboration (3:4; 4:1,11; 5:1). Most importantly, he wanted to provide for the ongoing life of the community by giving them instructions concerning *community ministry.* He instructed them both to minister and encourage one another and to respect the leaders who had been placed over them in the Lord. This would provide the unity and stability for the church to continue to grow in the absence of its founder.

Clues in the Context of 5:12-22

We've picked up some important clues along the way, but now we come to the heart of the mystery—the passage itself. How does this passage relate to the historical context of the letter and the immediate context of surrounding passages? Those who have overlooked some of the initial clues we have unearthed argue that this section is general in nature. They suggest that it contains only traditional material and instructions which Paul would have deemed necessary for any church of any generation. While it is possible that Paul may have used traditional phrases like "in everything give thanks," or "pray without ceasing," I think we will discover that the passage reflects a fresh composition designed to deal with the specific needs of the Thessalonian community.

First let's glance at the relationship between this passage and the rest of the letter. Proper behavior in the community is the recurring theme of the entire teaching section of this letter which begins at 4:1. Sexual purity was the first matter addressed. Notice it was related to community life with the phrase: "that no man transgress and defraud his brother (4:6)." Paul acknowledged that brotherly love was already being practiced, but he suggested that it could be improved upon. The insistence that they are "taught by God" (4:9) concerning brotherly love gives his instruction the full authority of God.

The discussion of the second coming enters at this point and continues to 5:11. It seems likely that Timothy had relayed to Paul the confusion in Thessalonica concerning this matter. Paul no doubt answered specific questions on the return of the Lord. The death of a believer prior to the second coming had caused such anxiety for some Thessalonians that the normal affairs of community life were being hindered. Interestingly, Paul focused even this discussion about the second coming on the matter of community living. He concluded the discussion with the exhortation that they should "comfort one another with these words" (4:18). Their natural curiosity concerning the second coming gave Paul further reason to insist that they strive for responsible and alert Christian conduct (5:6-11). All the problems they faced (harassment from their neighbors, attacks upon their founder, and internal dissensions) could best be met by the mutual encouragement one of another, and by loving recognition of those who have charge over them in the Lord. Thus verse 11 serves as a bridge closely linking the various concerns of the teaching section together with the picture of the ministering community. Everything is focused on undergirding the natural development of the ongoing life of the community.

Put yourself in Paul's shoes. Given the circumstances mentioned above, what would you have done to encourage this frightened and discouraged church? Your first priority would certainly have been to ensure for their continued care and ministry. You would want to encourage them to pull together and listen to those in charge. As we shall see, that was Paul's fundamental strategy.

The Work of Community Leaders

Notice that Paul addressed his remarks in 1 Thessalonians 5:12 to all community members. His first concern was that the members of the community give proper respect to their leaders. The fact that he had just exhorted them to "encourage one another and build one another up" did not alter the fact that there were those who were called to function as community leaders.

The use of the phrase "diligently labor" was probably intended to accent the magnitude of the intense physical exertion required of spiritual leaders. Furthermore it is likely that Paul used this phrase to describe the leaders who were worthy of high esteem. Simply put, those who are diligently laboring are the authentic leaders who deserve your respect. You should note that in 2 Thessalonians we are made aware that there were persons who wanted to exercise leadership influence but who were not laboring. These men had become a disturbance to the community and their presence had created confusion and difficulty for the authentic leaders.

The thrust of verses 12 and 13 is clear. There were certain individuals in Thessalonica who needed the brethren's recognition and highest esteem in love for the successful completion of their ministry on behalf of the entire community. Paul insisted that they deserved recognition and esteem because of their work. Paul used the terms "labor among you," "have charge over you," and "give you instruction" to describe the scope of their ministry. These terms are governed by a single article in the Greek. Thus they do not depict three separate ministries or three groups of persons. They are general terms chosen to convey a certain range of leadership activities which were being accomplished for the good of the community.

The addition of the phrase "live in peace with one another" recalled the unifying theme of this whole letter. Paul's overarching desire was to establish harmony in the community so they could encourage one another in the face of persecution and the community could command the respect of the outsiders (4:12). It is only in the atmosphere of peace that the members of the church, including the leaders, can accomplish their work unhindered. We should not overlook that the call to peace, while a general admonition, likely suggests that there was unrest between some of the brethren and those who were over them in the Lord.

We don't have to look far in our own experience to testify to the truth that where church members do not love and highly esteem their leaders, little work is accomplished for the Lord. Needless to say, that church's testimony in the community is hindered. It seems that every association has a church where there is a constant parade of preachers. None of them stay very long. They all leave for different reasons. One preaches too long, the other too loud. One is too authoritative, the next has no leadership ability. At the heart of the matter is the fact that the church does not esteem them in love and thus whoever comes as pastor will be ineffective. A word of balance to the pastors. Remember the phrase "diligently labor among you" is used to describe the pastors who are worthy of esteem. All too often our churches fail to respond because a pastor is too lazy to lead.

As previously noted, the term *labor* conveys the extent of the exertion. The next two descriptive words view those who "labor" from the vantage point of function. The first function described by the Greek word *proistemi* has been variously translated as (1) "preside," "lead," or (2) "protect," and "care for." In the Pastoral Letters the work of the bishops and elders is described with the use of this term. Their functions in the church are then compared with their duty as the head of the home (see 1 Tim. 3:4-5). This Greek word has a varied use both in the New Testament and in the ordinary language of the times. Nevertheless, the word alone seems most literally to convey some idea of "standing before" or "leading" unless the context dictates otherwise.

The context here seems actually to favor the concept of leading since Paul was pointing out to the brethren the need to respect certain identifiable persons who function in a unique leadership capacity in their behalf. Nevertheless, the function of leading, includes the idea of "caring for" (see 1 Thess. 2:7-8) and thus both senses of the word are probably in view. Any leader, pastor, or otherwise, would do well to remember that authority to lead is integrally tied to one's care for those under him. The phrase "in the Lord" is intentionally attached to this word to place a boundary on the leadership authority. Leadership takes place by the authority of the Lord and in the realm of spiritual affairs.

The final word describing the work of the leader is a word which suggests "warning" and "correction." It is the idea of a well-meaning earnestness with which one seeks to influence the mind and disposition of another by appropriate instruction, exhortation, warning, and correction. It is likely that we have here an early description of a community leader that we would now call the pastor. Notice that an official title was not a major concern for Paul. We seem to be title conscious today. An individual can claim whatever title he likes, but if the biblical functions of pastoral leadership are not being accomplished, the title has little significance. The leader here in 1 Thessalonians was described only by his task as he was to labor among, provide administrative leadership, and instruction. These three functions are still central to the work of the pastor.

We must renew our commitment to the biblical priorities. The church must allow the leader to provide that visionary leadership which gives direction to its ministry. Unfortunately some churches treat the pastor as a hireling who is given little to say in the direction of the church's ministry. Often these churches flounder around without a clear strategy for ministry. In the same manner, pastors must not attempt to exert this authority in a strong-handed manner. They must earn it by "laboring among" and "caring for the flock." The mission of the church is too vital to allow conflict between laity and staff. We must esteem one another highly in love that we might have a peaceful and powerful ministry.

Now if we tie this verse to the suggested historical reconstruction I would suggest that the leaders whom Paul wanted the community to honor were "Jason and the brethren." Paul had spent considerable time with these men, no doubt with a view to preparing them for leadership in the ongoing life of the community. Much of the dissension after Paul's departure was related to accusations about Paul's behavior. "Jason and the brethren" quickly emerged as leaders and as champions of Paul's cause. Some who opposed Jason and the brethren had made it their business to spread their doubts about Paul's integrity. This had not only caused a general unrest, but had also led to an uncertainty on the part of many members as to whom they should believe, and thus, in a certain sense, whom they should follow.

Those members who caused the greatest part of the internal dissension are identified with the use of the Greek term *ataktoi* translated as "unruly." The *ataktos* word group is found in the New Testament only in the Thessalonian letters. Thus we can safely assume that this term has a particular significance in relation to that community. The only reference to the "unruly" in 1 Thessalonians occurs in 5:14, but they are probably in view in 4:9-12. The discussion in 2 Thessalonians 3:7-8 suggests that idleness about work was an element of their unruly behavior. The *ataktos* word group is used to refer to community members who were disobedient to Paul's teaching (2 Thess. 3:6), who were not working with their hands (2 Thess. 3:11; 1 Thess. 4:11) and who in their spare time had spread dissent in the community by behaving like busybodies (2 Thess. 3:11 and 1 Thess. 4:11). The cartoon character of Lucy in the "Peanuts" comic strip well illustrates this type of nagging, destructive personality type. These persons polarize people and destroy the unity of the fellowship.

Second Thessalonians concludes with a strong warning directed at those who were "unruly." If anyone refused to obey what was said in the letter, he should be ostracized—he is not to be looked on as an enemy, but warned as a brother (see 1 Thess. 5:14). If we identify the agitators with the "unruly," characterized by idleness, the use of "diligently labor" is particularly pointed. The true leaders are those laboring, not those who are spreading dissent in their idle time. Doesn't this hold true in the life of the church today?

There is a question we need to address. In what respect are those identified by the phrase those "laboring among you" to be looked at as leaders? While this question may not appear to be a major concern to you at this point, it is important for the understanding of the function of spiritual gifts. There are those who suggest that the New Testament church had no official leaders who were invested with power or authority by virtue of their office or appointment. Further, there are those who suggest that the distinctions that we make between laity and clergy are artificial. They argue that individuals served in the New Testament community according to their spiritual gifts and the idea of official leadership was not taught in the New Testament. This in turn has led to a further conclusion that no one can tell another person when or how they may exercise their gifts. When an individual was prompted by the Spirit, he was no longer in control and must act or speak.

In recent years we have seen a healthy and biblical emphasis on the shared ministry of staff and church members. I rejoice in this discovery. The biblical teaching on spiritual gifts will offer even greater encouragement to the layperson in ministry. We must not allow this discovery to unneccessarily depreciate the work of those men and women called out by God for leadership roles in the church. Let's allow these texts to speak for themselves and provide the healthy balance in these matters.

Instead of trying to reach any conclusions concerning the nature of New Testament leadership at this early juncture in our study and with such little evidence, let us simply underline the clear implications of this passage.

(1) Paul did direct special attention to specific individuals who were laboring in a unique capacity for the good of the community. Therefore, in some sense these men formed an entity which is distinguishable from the "brethren" as a whole. The fact that Paul found it necessary to ask the brethren to ac-

knowledge these men may indicate that they were not appointed in an official manner before Paul left. However, the lack of appointment may be explained by Paul's forced departure. The question of an official appointment is in a sense academic because this passage was intended to elicit the esteem of the community on behalf of these persons and thus functioned in a practical sense as an appointment of sorts.

(2) The attempt to distinguish between the selection of an individual for a task and the desire and "gifts" enabling one to serve is artificial. It must further be noted that Paul, in the present context, did not discuss the leaders or the brethren in terms of spiritual gifts. The very fact that we expect such a discussion here makes the silence even more meaningful.

(3) Recognition and acceptance by the community is vital to the success of these ministers and consequently to the well-being of the community. It is difficult, if not artificial, to draw a hard and fast line between the authorization of the community and the loving acceptance of the community. If the community does not esteem leaders in love, no amount of presumed authority will make their ministry effective.

(4) The emphasis here is on function or service. This is not to be used as an argument for or against "official ministry" in this passage. In later passages such as 1 Timothy 3:5 where the official nature of the leader is more readily discerned, the emphasis is still primarily on function.

(5) Paul exhorted all the brethren to minister (5:11-14), yet he encouraged the brethren to respect their "leaders," apparently seeing no contradiction in these two statements.

The Shared Ministry

In verse 14 Paul repeated the term *brethren* to draw attention to the responsibilities for ministry shared by everyone in the community. In 1 Thessalonians 5:11 Paul indicated his desire that the Thessalonians encourage and edify one another, and he made his exhortation clear by application to the specific needs of the community. The "unruly" were in special need of warning and correction. They must be brought back into line for the good of the community. The "disconsolate" may be a reference to those distressed by the delay of the coming of the Lord and/or the death of a friend. It could also refer to those depressed by the present afflictions of persecution. These persons need to be consoled and encouraged. The spiritually "weak" were those whose faith was shaky for any number of reasons. These persons must be clung to. It is so easy to allow the weak to slip through the cracks of our church fellowship.

The ministries mentioned here were tailored to the specific needs in Thessalonica. Verse 14 is concluded with the broad command to show patience to everyone, which in the present context means everyone in the church. Notice that patience has particular value for the unity of the ministering community. As our study unfolds you will see that the idea of patience will continually reoccur whenever we study a community ministry passage (1 Cor. 13:4; Rom. 12:10-12; and Eph. 4:2). Community ministry, by its very nature, requires patience. The church member who feels the need to criticize every program of the church, the child in the Sunday School class who requires constant attention, the single adult who feels his "needs aren't being met" all demand patience from the ministering community. It is part of the nature of the church to care patiently for all these needs. We too often expect uniformity of spiritual growth from our members. However, we are at different levels of spiritual maturity and thus need personalized and patient care.

When believers are working together in a community setting there will almost invariably be disagreements and the resulting tension. My wife and I form a ministry team of two to nurture and disciple our three daughters. Believe it or not, we do not always agree on methodology. We embrace the same goal and therefore we work together to that end. Thus we must exercise patience as we hammer out our differences.

In verse 15 Paul exhorted all members to oversee the ethical behavior of their fellow members. They must see to it that no one returns evil for evil. It is often suggested that Paul was concerned about

Christians retaliating against their persecutors. This is certainly possible. However, the first application is to the returning of evil for evil in the context of the Christian community.

Human nature is clearly reflected in the popular bumper sticker: "Don't get mad, get even." Tragically this attitude sometimes rears its ugly head in the fellowship of believers. It is probable that Paul specifically had in mind the tensions in the Thessalonian community related to the unruly. Thus the matter of conflicts within the community and afflictions from without are both brought to mind. Paul did not stop with the prohibition of retaliation. He demanded that they go beyond the neutral point of coexistence and seek the good for one another and for all persons. The Christian replaces that which is harmful by that which is ethically correct and has the best interests of his neighbor at heart (see Rom. 12:17-21). Redemptive behavior always requires that we take the initiative to minister to those who do evil to us. We overcome evil with good. It is easier to ignore the person who does us harm. It takes a humble spirit to seek reconciliation.

There has been a healthy return to an emphasis on the ministry of the laity. This passage gives us further cause to ensure that it is implemented in our churches. We must view the staff and the laity as a ministry team. The leaders are responsible for caring, teaching, and administrating, but all the members together are called to build up the fellowship of the church. Notice that many of the duties that we have often felt to be the private domain of the pastor are in fact commanded of all the brethren. Have you ever found yourself thinking, *Fred and Mary haven't been here lately? I bet they are having problems. The pastor ought to go by and encourage them.* Could it be that God is calling you to do that?

Worship and the Ministry Community

It is possible that verses 16-18 contain teachings derived from traditional teaching material. Phrases like "pray without ceasing" and "rejoice always" are common in the New Testament. Yet one must ask, are these injunctions simply general statements with no specific purpose, or did Paul include them here for a particular reason? This entire section (5:12-22) deals with the ongoing life of the community. It is therefore difficult to imagine that Paul would intentionally interrupt an otherwise unified passage with unrelated injunctions. Paul had just shown in the preceding discussion how unity achieved through mutual care combats both external and internal difficulties. Now Paul pointed them to the source of power for ministry.

The act of gathered worship is essential to the ongoing life of the community. Paul exhorted them to rejoice always, even in adversity, pray unceasingly, and give thanks. While these are general phrases, the context suggests that Paul was referring to worship activities. The source of divine power is tapped as the community gathers for worship. In the same process the community is knit together and built up from within. The discussion of a ministering community would not be complete without this focus on gathered worship. Thus even these seemingly general instructions have a specific concern. We would do well to notice that the ministering church is empowered in the context of worship. The psalmist told us that God inhabits the praise of His people.

It is refreshing that many churches are rediscovering the strength derived from effective worship. Worship must not be allowed to degenerate into a repetitive and dull ritual which must be tolerated weekly. Every member must come prepared to encounter the living God. The pastor is responsible for providing meaningful opportunities for worship. This requires more than selecting a few hymns and typing an order of service. It is worth the effort if one desires a church family empowered for ministry.

Prophecy in the Community

Verses 19-22 have elicited much comment. It is necessary in the context to appeal for the removal of the "Corinthian spectacles." Interpreters have almost unanimously approached this passage with 1 Corinthians 12—14 embedded in their minds. We cannot assume that the community at Thessalonica resembled the church at Corinth with respect to the spiritual gifts. We must not assume that their worship experience was plagued with the abuses obvious in 1 Corinthians 14. We must evaluate 1 Thessalonians on the basis on the actual evidence presented by the letter itself.

Before we attempt to relate this section to the historical context, we must determine what the text itself says. The short phrase "Do not quench the Spirit" has been understood in two very different ways. It has been taken as a very general statement which may have in view such matters as idleness, immorality, negligence of the daily stirring up of the Spirit, or attempting to resist evil by natural means. The major objection to this view is the context, particularly the mention of prophecy in verse 20. A majority of commentators have argued that the reference is to all the gifts of the Spirit. Some who would agree that Paul was dealing here with all the gifts maintain that he was mainly concerned with tongues or prophecy.

I find no evidence that suggests "Do not quench the Spirit" refers to the presence of a variety of spiritual manifestations. I would point out that there is no clear reference in either letter, nor specifically in the present context, which indicated the presence of ecstatic gifts such as tongues in Thessalonica. I am using *ecstatic* at this point to refer to an emotional or psychological state where an individual is no longer in control. Further, there is no reference to a variety of gifts, ecstatic or otherwise. The abilities which we presume would be required by the leaders here are certainly similar to manifestations which in later letters are referred to as spiritual gifts, but they are not treated as such here. The only spiritual gift of which we are made fully aware is prophetic utterance, and even it is not discussed in terms of a spiritual gift. There is no reason to suspect that the Thessalonians would have understood "Spirit" as a reference to all spiritual gifts.

In the same way it has been argued that in 2 Thessalonians 2:2 *pneuma* (spirit) refers to ecstatic speech, and therefore may point to the presence of tongues in Thessalonica. However a closer look will make it clear that Paul there had in mind a verbal revelation with clear content, as is made obvious in verse 2c. Thus, at best, *pneuma* (spirit) may refer to prophecy uttered in an ecstatic state of mind, but it probably refers to prophecy, without any indication of the psychological state of the prophet. The arguments which appeal to various

Corinthian texts are not valid. Those texts tell us nothing about the situation in Thessalonica. The terminology used in 1 Corinthians must be understood in the light of that historical situation. Notice that there is a tendency to assume for this early text what we find in later correspondence.

In spite of the overwhelming agreement among many commentators that Paul had in mind all the spiritual gifts, I think that verses 19-22 form a unit in which Paul dealt only with prophetic utterance. At this point we have looked at too little evidence to attempt to give a detailed description of New Testament prophecy. For clarity, I am using *prophecy* in a broad sense to refer to an intelligible spoken message, given under inspiration, whose content is from the Lord. Verses 19 and 20 are parallel, and thus verse 20 explains verse 19. There were apparently various "prophetic voices" in Thessalonica, and not all of them had proved to be accurate as 2 Thessalonians 2:2 clearly shows. If the Thessalonians responded to the prophetic confusion by despairing of all prophecy, they would forfeit the benefit to be derived from authentic prophecy. Paul therefore combined the exhortation "Do not despise prophetic utterances" with "Do not quench the Spirit" to underline the importance—the divine necessity —of listening to those who speak an authentic message from the Lord. The verbs are present imperatives which may indicate that the Thessalonians were already guilty of quenching the Spirit in this regard. They must immediately cease this behavior and, for the welfare of the community, heed the authentic prophetic messages.

Anytime there is a scandal involving a pastor or television evangelist, there are those who want to lump all preachers together and dismiss them. We can readily see how wrong and disasterous this would be to the life of the church. However, it gives us some sensitivity to the danger Paul sensed in Thessalonica where someone had wrongly prophesied that the Lord had already come.

Paul feared the disastrous results of a wholesale rejection of prophetic speech, but he was equally aware that the possibility of false prophetic utterance made unquestioning acceptance of all "prophetic" speech unsatisfactory. Therefore Paul exhorted them to "examine" everything. Though the terminology of verses 21-22 is general, the context rules against the suggestion that "examine everything" is a universal principle intended to embrace all of the Christian life. On the other hand, the suggestion that it means examine all spiritual gifts is equally unsatisfactory since it assumes a situation like that of Corinth. The flow of the argument suggests that "Examine every thing" has in view the *content* of all prophetic utterances; whether they be moral exhortation or speculation about the day of the Lord. Presumably all the brethren were encouraged to do the approving of the prophetic utterances. The present context does not indicate that Paul had in mind a particular gift by which some are qualified to judge the message of the prophets. Notice that the emphasis on judging was first of all optimistic. The good prophetic utterances were to be maintained, but every bad kind of prophetic utterance must be rejected.

Did Paul give the Thessalonians any criterion for evaluating the prophetic utterances? There are scholars who have argued that the word *good* be translated as "genuine." In this case Paul would be referring to a testing which determines the source and nature of the inspired utterance. Others argue that *good* means "ethically right" or "beneficial" and that this is the yardstick for measuring prophecy. The present text does not provide sufficient evidence for us to draw any absolute conclusions concerning how to evaluate prophetic utterance.

What then is the relationship of this unit of thought to the passage as a whole and to the historical context? It is at once apparent that Paul dealt throughout verses 12-22 with the functions of the ministering community. I think that there is a specific connection with 5:12-13. Paul was aware that the growing suspicion concerning prophetic utterance could render ineffective the ministry of Jason and other authentic leaders in the community. Paul must therefore encourage the Thessalonians to heed the word of God given through the called leaders. These men could be clearly identified by their hard labor, their ministry on behalf of the church and their ethical life-styles. The brethren must utilize spiritual discernment so that they would not ignore those truly called by God to lead the community.

Assimilating the Clues

It's time for us to see if we can begin to form some preliminary conclusions based on our study of 1 Thessalonians alone. These should form the foundation for our understanding of spiritual gifts, but we must be careful not to allow our minds to leap ahead to what we "know" (or at least "think" we know) to be in 1 Corinthians 12—14.

1. This passage was written in response to a particular and unique historical situation. The Thessalonians were facing affliction from without and dissensions from within. Paul encouraged them in many areas of spiritual growth, but more importantly he focused on unique role of the ministering community made up of leaders and brethren who were to minister together.

2. The almost total absence of what today is referred to as spiritual gifts is most important. Notice that prophecy, skills for leadership, and the responsibility for all to minister are all discussed here, but not in terms of *spiritual gifts*. Why did Paul not uphold the leaders on the basis of their spiritual gifts as he would do later in 1 Corinthians 12:28 and Ephesians 4:11? Why did he not insist that every member should serve based on the *spiritual* gift given them for this purpose? This is certainly the theme of later passages such as 1 Corinthians 12:7,-11; Romans 12:3,6; and Ephesians 4:7,16? Its absence here should not be overlooked.

3. Several distinct and important teachings which will be found in all subsequent passages concerning the ministering community are conspiciously lacking here.

    (a) The idea that every believer is gifted to serve would have been helpful in this passage. Paul then could have encouraged the brethren to minister to the unruly and others based on the truth that they had all received a specific gift for ministry.

(b) There is no discussion of the source, nature, and purpose of the gifts for ministry. Why is there no list of gifts?

(c) There is no insistence that the community needed a diversity of gifts for complete ministry. In that same light, there is no comparison of the ministering community to the human *body*.

4. While lacking the language of spiritual gifts, several ideas which will be fully developed in later community ministry passages are clearly present. Please note and remember these.

(a) Paul insisted that every member is responsible for the ministry in the community. Every member is concerned for his brother's spiritual welfare, including his ethical behavior. This is a truth that we must apply to the ministry of our local church. God's intention for the church was and is for a shared ministry. Paul declared that unity and peace will be the result of every-member ministry.

(b) Even though all members must minister, God has called out some individuals for leadership functions and they must be esteemed for their hard labor. Two primary functions of these leaders become clear: oversight or administration of the ministry and instruction of the brethren.

(c) It is likely that there is some relationship between the leading of the community and the empowering of the Spirit. This is suggested by the phrase, "Do not quench the Spirit." In that light, keep in mind that the Thessalonian believers were told to evaluate all prophetic utterance.

You might already have begun to ask with me, "Why is there no mention of spiritual gifts in this community ministry passage?" Arguments from silence are always difficult. It might very simply be that the situation in Thessalonica was not as volatile as that of 1 Corinthians and thus there was no need to discuss the *gifts*. Later when we investigate Romans and Ephesians, we will find a discussion of *gifts*. There is nothing in either of those letters to suggest that there was any problem related to gifts. Why then did Paul include a discussion of gifts in Romans and Ephesians and not in 1 Thessalonians? Why is there no mention of the ecstatic or miraculous gifts such as tongues in Thessalonica? Is it possible that there were none in Thessalonica? While we have gained some valuable insights in our study of 1 Thessalonians, we have been left with a number of important questions. This very naturally leads us to 1 Corinthians with great anticipation. Keep an open mind and open Bible.

2
Identifying the Spirituals

Interesting that Paul's troubles did not come from heathens but so-called spirituals.

If I were to tell you that the First Church of Corinth was looking for a pastor and I knew an influential member of the pulpit committee, would you want me to put your name before them? "Don't do me any favors," you say. I thought you might feel that way. I have asked that question at enough pastor's conferences to have anticipated your response.

After all, who is looking for a church with splinter groups with some claiming Paul, others Apollos, Cephas, or Christ? A church with one split is bad enough, but who wants to tackle one with a four-way split? The other incidental problems are a little troublesome as well. It really shouldn't bother a prospective pastor that a man is living with his father's wife! It is a little troubling that certain members of the community are proud of it. At least there is an element in the church that balances this sexual immorality. They tell me that some married couples have decided to live a celibate marriage. It is not altogether clear that both parties are happy about the arrangement.

You can be sure the church was well known in the community since members are suing one another in court. It seems that everybody is fighting for their rights, whether it's the freedom to dine in a pagan temple or for the women to speak in the assembly with their heads uncovered. The whole community is still talking about the last time the church celebrated the Lord's Supper. Word has it that while some left hungry, others were a little tipsy from the communion wine. Perhaps I should mention in passing that the Corinthians seem to be

40

thoroughly confused about the matter of spiritual gifts. There are some who think they speak with the tongues of angels. They claim to have an abundance of all gifts. At the same time there are others who think they have no gifts. Can that be?

Not many folks would voluntarily tackle such a church. We would see it as a bomb with a lighted fuse. I find it singularly fascinating that many folks turn to Corinthians, without fully understanding its problems, to develop their theology of spiritual gifts. Passages are lifted out of the immediate and historical context and used to defend an existing practice in a particular church. Or conversely another passage is lifted from the same context to argue against a practice. For example, I find people who love to quote the first verse of 1 Corinthians 14:5, "Now I wish that you all spoke in tongues." They then conclude that all Christians must speak in tongues. But I find another group who likes to point to 1 Corinthians 14:23 and ask, "Will they not declare that you are mad?" They insist that tongues are at best a nuisance. How can we reach both conclusions from the same chapter?

The detailed and lengthy discussion of spiritual gifts in 1 Corinthians demands that we concentrate on this letter in order to understand spiritual gifts. Yet we must pay close attention to the Corinthian situation and distinguish between basic principles and corrections of abuses at Corinth. Many commentators do not give sufficient attention to the central role that the spiritual gifts play in the difficulties plaguing the Corinthian community.

Paul's introductory paragraph often alerts the leader to the central issue of a letter. We should notice that the first matter which Paul addressed in this letter was the abundance of spiritual gifts possessed by the community. This comes prior to his mention of the existence of various factions within the church. The emphasis on the abundance of gifts is particularly apparent in 1:5-7. It is likely that Paul echoed the claims of some in Corinth when he wrote: "In *everything* you were enriched in Him, in *all* speech and in *all* knowledge, . . . so that you are *not* lacking in *any* gift" (author's italics). While Paul cited this boast of abundance without any corrective at this point, he would later remind them that they didn't yet possess *all* knowledge, nor did any of them possess all gifts.

From the Acts account of the Corinthian ministry (Acts 18:1-17), we find that Paul stayed in Corinth about eighteen months: long enough to establish a sizeable congregation. From Acts we would conclude that the Christian community in Corinth was made up of God-fearers as well as Jews and Gentiles (18:4,6-7). God-fearers refers to Gentiles who had accepted the basic teachings of Judaism, but had not gone through the necessary steps to become Jewish converts.

Between The Visit And The Letter

It is difficult to reconstruct the sequence of events that occurred after Paul's visit and prior to the writing of 1 Corinthians, a period of 15 to 27 months.[1] According to Acts, Apollos visited Corinth during this period (18:24 to 19:1). It is possible that Apollos's teaching had indirectly contributed to some of the confusion in Corinth. Apparently some claimed him as their spiritual leader (1 Cor. 1:12). Some commentators suggest that Apollos contributed to the quest for knowledge and wisdom, but the evidence in 1 Corinthians does not indicate that Paul felt any animosity toward Apollos (3:1-9; 4:6; 16:-12). It is doubtful that we will find here the major cause of Corinthian problems. While it appears that some Corinthians claimed Peter as their spiritual leader, it is uncertain that Peter actually visited Corinth. The two letters taken together indicate that there had been numerous wise teachers to visit Corinth (1 Cor. 4:15,19; 2 Cor. 10:10 *ff.*). No doubt some of the teaching subsequent to Paul's visit had played a role in the Corinthian confusion.

According to 1 Corinthians 5:9, Paul had written one letter prior to 1 Corinthians. The letter seemingly dealt with immorality in the church, but it had been misunderstood by the Corinthians. The actual writing of 1 Corinthians was prompted by inquiries from the Corinthian community. Notice the repetition of a form of the phrase "Now concerning the things about which you wrote" (7:1,25; 8:1; 12:1; 16:1,12). We don't know whether the inquiries came from the entire community or from a group in that community that was still faithful to Paul. Apart from the inquiries, we are told that Paul had received disturbing reports from "Chloe's people" (1:11; 5:1; 11:18). Therefore Paul's answers to certain questions may well reflect not only the Corinthian inquiry, but the information from the reports Paul had received concerning the state of affairs at Corinth.

The wealth of information supplied by 1 Corinthians has produced numerous reconstructions of the historical situation. While this warns us about being dogmatic about our description of the situation, it does not excuse us from the task. Accurate interpretation depends on a clear understanding of the historical situation. I have found it most helpful to allow the Corinthian letter itself to describe the situation.

The Spirituals In Corinth

The presence of the party names in 1 Corinthians 1:12 has caused many commentators to try to explain the Corinthians difficulties by describing the various parties. This approach always seems to flounder on the lack of information about the parties or the issues. Secondly, the letter suggests a friendly relationship between Paul and Apollos (3:4-9; 4:6). While the presence of one or more organized factions is doubtful, one can detect in Corinth a number of individuals who, to some extent, shared certain similarities of belief and practice.

Who Were The Spirituals?

At the very heart of the Corinthian difficulties is the conviction by some that they were *pneumatikoi*—"spirituals" or "spiritual persons." *Pneumatikos* is from the root word *pneuma* which means "spirit." Fifteen of the twenty-four occurrences of *pneumatikos* in the Pauline epistles are found in Corinthians. Because Paul used this term to refer to a group of folk in the Corinthian community, I will follow suit and simply call them "spirituals." Notice that in five occasions in 1 Corinthians *pneumatikos* refers to spiritual persons (2:13-15; 3:1; 12:1; 14:37) and frequently there is a polemical overtone. Not all English translations will render *pneumatikos* as "spiritual persons" in 2:13. I believe the context favors this wording: "interpreting spiritual truths to spiritual men." About 12:1, see discussion about that verse.

1:10
1:52

It appears that at the time of Paul's writing this was not a well-defined group of persons with a developed set of beliefs. Their spiritual enthusiasm had emerged in relation to a number of possible factors such as outside influences, the social environment of Corinth, misunderstanding of Pauline teaching, and the spontaneous religious zeal which may have accompanied religious conversion during this time. It is likely that the spiritual enthusiasm in Corinth had developed out of a haphazard interplay of numerous factors and was not organized or unified even in teaching. This is not unlike the growth of the charismatic movement in recent years.

The Role of Wisdom

Those who believed themselves to be "spirituals" claimed to possess special wisdom (1:18 *ff.*; 2:6 *ff.*; 12:8) and knowledge (1:5; 8:1; 12:8). They apparently believed that their wisdom gave them a special insight into the mysteries of God's plan (2:6-9*a* and especially 13:2). Paul corrected their arrogant claim to a deep wisdom by insisting that their wisdom was earthly and was foolishness before God (3:18-19). The most important corrective passage concerning wisdom is 2:6-16. In this passage Paul utilized the spiritual's vocabulary to demonstrate the content of true wisdom. This redefinition of wisdom effectively refuted the claim of the spirituals to possess a deeper wisdom. Paul redefined the true spiritual person as one who had received the word of the cross. The true spiritual person would therefore recognize the things *freely given him by God* (2:12). This phrase translates a Greek word with the root *charis* (grace). This stress on the recognition of grace will recur throughout this letter as the principle to correct the arrogant boasting of the spirituals.

The spirituals apparently believed that Paul's teaching lacked deep spiritual insight. Paul insisted that he shared spiritual things with spiritual men (2:14). The corrective impact of this statement is obvious in 3:1 where Paul bluntly declared: "And I, brethren, could not speak to you as spiritual men, but as to men of flesh as to babes in Christ." It was not that Paul was unable to communicate true wisdom. Their immaturity had caused them not to comprehend the true wisdom of the cross. Thus Paul corrected their claim to special wisdom by contrasting the deeper wisdom of the cross, which would itself eliminate all boasting. This would in turn stop the foolish strife they had created as they had clamored for one leader after the other (3:3-4).

We Possess All Knowledge

The spirituals also claimed to possess all "knowledge" (*gnōsis*). By knowledge it appears that they meant a special insight into the realities of Christian existence in the here and now. On one occasion, a claim to knowledge, had been used to justify behavior which had created difficulties in the church (see ch. 8). It is likely that Paul simply echoed their boast in 8:1; "We know that we have all knowledge" (cf. 1:5; 13:2). On the basis of their knowledge, the spirituals had concluded that idols were nothing (8:4) and thus decided that eating meat offered to idols was of no consequence. Paul countered that their knowledge was not as complete as they thought. "If anyone supposes that he knows anything, he has not yet known as he ought to know" (8:2). True knowledge would have led to loving, edifying behavior toward the brethren, but their knowledge had resulted only in arrogance.

The Spirituals and the Lord's Supper

The three occurrences of the term *spiritual* in 10:3-4 should not go unnoticed. The spirituals had a crude, almost magical view of baptism and the Lord's Supper (1:12 *ff.* and ch. 10). Paul argued that the Israelites were baptized into Moses, had eaten *spiritual* food and had drunk *spiritual* drink, which was from the *spiritual* rock. Yet because of their behavior, they were laid low in the wilderness. These things occurred as an example and should serve as a warning against spiritual arrogance. This magical view of the Lord's Supper (11:17 *ff.*) had created critical problems in the community. They had neglected the purpose and meaning of the love feast or fellowship meal which preceded the actual Lord's Supper. Instead of drawing the community members into close fellowship and responsible behavior, it had led to further dissension. Paul called them to edifying behavior in the context of their community.

This idea may, at first, seem foreign to us, but let's look at it more closely. There are those who think that if they walk the church aisle and are baptized, this alone will put them right with God. The belief that any religious activity not accompanied by true repentance and conversion can put a person in right standing with God demonstrates a type of magical view of the religious activity itself. We see this expressed subtly when people think they can behave as they wish if they attend church regularly or be faithful for the Lord's Supper or Mass.

The Spirituals and Spiritual Gifts

There are three extremely important occurrences of *pneumatikos* (spiritual) in 1 Corinthians 12-14. These will be dealt with in great detail later. Since it is likely that no precise system of teaching had yet emerged among the spirituals, the spiritual gifts were of tremendous significance. They provided a sure and visible sign that one was spiritual. "We can speak the language of the angels! We have all knowledge!" Thus it should be no surprise to us that the spirituals were particularly zealous to possess and display spiritual gifts. It is equally understandable that the more dramatic and more visible gifts were most highly prized.

Overrealized Eschatalogy

Chapter 15 is important for the proper understanding of the Corinthian difficulties. Notice that in 15:44-46 *pneumatikos* occurs four times in a context which suggests that Paul found it necessary to correct an "overrealized" eschatology. Hang on, I know that's a fifty-cent phrase. Primarily it means that some Corinthians believed that they already possessed all of the supernatural powers and blessings which heaven had to offer. This mistaken idea is reflected earlier in the letter when Paul summarized their belief about their spiritual status: "You are already filled, you have already become rich, you have become kings without us" (1 Cor. 4:8).

We find a similar misunderstanding in a slightly more subtle form in our day. One does not have to watch long on some of the television worship services to hear the preacher proclaim the kingdom of God has already come. There is no reason that a Christian should be sick, suffer discouragement, or be poor. An overrealized eschatology is at the very heart of the health, wealth, and success gospel. It fails to give full weight to the effect of this fallen present world.

To correct this false teaching Paul emphasized that the present body was perishable, sown in dishonor, sown in weakness, sown as a natural body. They had no place for weakness or dishonor! On the other hand, the resurrected body will be raised in glory, raised in power, raised a spiritual body. Paul was well aware that the spirituals were claiming that they were *already* participants in the full glory and power of the Lord. Paul conceded that there is a spiritual body (15:44), but that it is not first—it must follow the natural (15:46). The fact that the natural is first seems obvious to us. Without a clear understanding of the Corinthian overrealized eschatology, we might wonder why Paul would state a truth that is so clear. Further, you should notice that Paul again concluded this section with an emphasis on responsible Christian behavior in the present. "Therefore my beloved brethren, be steadfast, immovable, always abounding in the work of the Lord" (15:58). To quote a popular little phrase: "They were so heavenly minded, they were no earthly good." Paul exhorted them to come back to earth and be steadfast in the work of the Lord.

The Problem of Arrogance

There are a few other terms which are used frequently in 1 Corinthians to describe the immature behavior of the spirituals. Two word groups with closely related meanings are *phusioō* (puff up, make arrogant) and *kauchaomai* (boast, glory). Six of the seven occurrences of *phusioō* are found in 1 Corinthians and thirty-five of the fifty-three uses of *kauchaomai* are found here, but the contextual significance is far more important than mere statistics. The spirituals were puffed-up and they boasted because of those things which they possessed— the spiritual gifts. They were *already* filled, *already* rich and therefore they boasted that they *already* reigned. Paul rebuked their boasting (4:7) by asking very simply what they possessed that they did not receive. Please note once again the cure for spiritual arrogance is an understanding of the graciousness of God!

An immature overevaluation of spiritual gifts, particularly those relating to speech, and revelation had led to a boasting in people (3:21, *kauchaomai*). Their arrogant (*phusioō,* 4:6) comparison of one wise teacher with another had led to confusion even among the spirituals. It is possible that some of the spirituals were actually claiming to belong to Paul, Apollos, or Cephas. The use of the various names served to demonstrate the disunity and immature overevaluation of human teachers among the spirituals. They were eager to respond to the "next" leader who demonstrated greater spectacular gifts or gave them wiser teaching based on a revelation given in a vision. It was this sort of attitude that led some to doubt Paul's apostolic authority. Paul was forced to address this in strong language again in 2 Corinthians 10—13.

In 1 Corinthians 4:6 Paul stated that he had applied these truths about leaders to Apollos and himself in a figurative way in order that "no one of you might become arrogant in behalf of one against the other." This immature zeal for wise leaders and the resulting disunity indicated the absurdity of their claim to be spirituals (3:1-4).

Although there was no organized group of opponents, Paul did face opposition in Corinth. The spirituals, on the basis of their spiritual gifts, had placed themselves and their leaders above Paul. In their estimation Paul was lacking in wisdom and dramatic gifts (2:1; 4:9 *ff.* and see the discussion of 12:22 *ff.* below). Paul reminded them that no matter how many teachers they might have, he was still their father (4:15). He then issued a warning to those behaving arrogantly (*phusi- oō*), as though he were not coming, that he would soon come and test their powers.

The Issue of Freedom

The spirituals were also arrogant concerning the freedom which their elevated status gave them. Their understanding of freedom is well reflected by their slogan, "All things are lawful" (6:12; 10:23). They believed that their freedom had lifted them above normal Christian morality, tradition, and sexual role distinctions. Their exalted status had made irrelevant or even praiseworthy such bodily activities as sexual immorality. One flagrant case of immorality is given particular attention. A member of the community was apparently living with his stepmother in an incestuous relationship. Paul was horrified by the fact that some have become arrogant (*phusioō*, 5:2) concerning this relationship. It appears that this relationship was common knowledge in the Christian community. There had been no attempt to conceal it. On the contrary, some had boasted (*kauchaomai*, 5:6) about it because it demonstrated how completely the spirituals had been freed from the moral restrictions of conventional religious life. While, at first, it seems impossible to think that someone would boast concerning sexual sin, we still see people today who believe that their spirituality places them above God's law. Sexual abberation was apparently prevalent in the cultic following of Jim Jones.

When you read this entire letter, you may be surprised to discover that another sexual problem involves an ascetic tendency, that is to say, an avoidance of physical pleasure such as sex. It seems likely that some of the spirituals had adopted as ascetic life-style, even though married, to demonstrate their exalted status and to show their freedom from bodily needs (1 Cor. 7:5).

There are other curious problems that emerge from this arrogant insistence on freedom. The matter of eating idol meat or attending a service at a pagan temple was, for some, an issue of freedom. The right of a woman to pray or prophesy in public had almost certainly become an issue of freedom for some of the spirituals intent upon making a public statement.[2] Paul corrected their demand for *freedom at any cost* with his insistence that the mature spiritual person would surrender personal freedom for the winning of souls and the needs of others (ch. 9).

The Role of Religious Zeal

One final word group which appears to be particularly meaningful in understanding the Corinthian community is the *zeloō* (zealous) word group. This term accurately described the youthful and often immature enthusiasm of this community. Their misguided zeal led them to a jealous bickering over spiritual leaders. Interestingly in 2 Corinthians 7:7 the repentant Corinthians are said to have renewed their zeal for Paul. Their zeal was such that it could lead them from one extreme to the other. They act like spiritual Ping-Pong balls. For our purposes it is important to notice that the Corinthians were zealous for the spiritual gifts (1 Cor. 12:31; 14:1,12,39). Paul could say without hesitation: "Since you are zealous of spiritual gifts" (1 Cor. 14:12).

[margin note: All directions at once.]

Paul was faced with a dilemma. He did not want to quench the spiritual enthusiasm of this young community, but he did want to correct it and redirect it toward more mature ends. My dad used to say that as a pastor he wasn't sure whether it was easier to warm up a corpse or cool down a zealot. Paul may well have faced both problems in this community. It is obvious there were some folks who were zealous for gifts, for spiritual leaders and their own rights. It is likely that others had responded to the immature zeal of the spirituals with a calculating coolness. How can we bring the two together and correct both errors?

[margin note: Paul wrote to redefine a Sp. person!]

Summary—A Final Word

I suggest that the difficulties in Corinth are to be traced to a spiritual enthusiasm which probably did not possess a developed set of teachings nor show any real unity. This spiritual enthusiasm had emerged in relation to numerous possible factors such as the environment of Corinth, outside influences and a spontaneous religious zeal which accompanied religious conversion. Therefore I think it is possible to understand this letter as Paul's redefining of the spiritual person. The truly spiritual person will recognize that all is of grace (2:12), and therefore will find no grounds for boasting in any gift.

[margin note at bottom: 2 marks of Sp. person:
1) Acknowledges all is of grace.
2) Lives by law of love.]

Secondly and closely related, the spiritual person is one whose behavior is determined by love.

There are several considerations which must be kept in mind as we work our way through 1 Corinthians 12—14. The historical context we have just discussed and the significance of the spiritual gifts must always be kept in focus during the study of these chapters. First Corinthians 12—14 is not, therefore, to be viewed as an isolated, unemotional, theological treatment of spiritual gifts, but as an intensely personal, robustly original and fundamentally positive evaluation of spiritual gifts for the empowering of the New Testament church.

While it is true that Paul's evaluation of the role of spiritual gifts was basically positive (12:11), we cannot overlook that Paul's appraisal was placed against an abberant understanding of gifts in Corinth and the resulting practical difficulties. For that reason we must pay close attention to Paul's style of argument, especially the subtle nuances of correction. It is necessary that we concentrate on the central thrust of Paul's argument rather than becoming sidetracked over an issue that particularly engages our interest. This is especially important in chapter 14 where it can sometimes appear that Paul seemed, at best, to vacillate in his evaluation of tongues. Therefore we will attempt not to focus on such matters as the description of a particular gift and miss the flow of the chapter. These may be items of interest, but they are not the major concern of this book.

To fully understand Paul's assessment of spiritual gifts we must treat 1 Corinthians 12—14 as a unified whole. All too often commentaries seem to treat 1 Corinthians 13 as a separate entity. We will discover that it is at the heart of Paul's corrective. Chapter 12 contains a positive redefinition and broadening of the understanding of spiritual gifts. Chapter 13 is not only integral to the argument of these three chapters, but is central to the entire letter. Paul did not suggest that love is a way superior to gifts, nor did he dub love the highest gift, nor even establish love as the means for evaluating gifts. Here he effectively and systematically redefined the "spiritual man." It is on the basis of this redefinition of the spiritual man that Paul would develop in chapter 14 practical guidelines for seeking and using spiritual gifts in the church. "So also you, since you are zealous of spiritual gifts, seek to abound for the edification of the church."

Notes

1. C.K. Barrett, *A Commentary on the First Epistle to the Corinthians,* Harper's New Testament Commentaries, (New York: Harper and Row, Publishers, 1968), p. 8.
2. I will give full comment on women praying and prophesying in my discussion of 1 Corinthians 14:33.

3
Redefining the Spiritual Gifts

What's the Question?

The first three verses of this section (1 Cor. 12:1-3) are exciting to say the least. It is commonly agreed that "Now concerning spiritual gifts" signifies that Paul was referring to another inquiry from the Corinthian community. That's the easy part! Now, what was the question or questions? It is significant that the Corinthians had found it necessary to ask Paul's opinion about the spiritual gifts. Had Paul left them ignorant concerning this matter, or had teachers subsequent to Paul created such confusion that they needed a fresh reminder concerning Paul's position on these matters?

We should also notice that it was this inquiry, arising out of a historical situation with abundant but misunderstood spiritual gifts, that presented the opportunity and provided the catalyst for the emergence of Paul's *first* and *most comprehensive* treatment of *spiritual gifts.* The principles developed here would form the basis for the teaching of Romans 12 and Ephesians 4. Previously, in 1 Thessalonians, Paul formulated concepts similar to those found in this section; but it is here in this highly charged atmosphere where Paul first enunciated the language and principles of spiritual gifts.

Back to the question! Our reconstruction of the question depends on a decision concerning the gender of *(tōn pneumatikōn)* "spiritual gifts" in verse 1. It can be taken as a masculine (spiritual persons) or as neuter (spiritual gifts). Many translations render it as a neuter because of the discussion which follows and because of a similar usage

53

in 14:1. Yet, as we have previously noted, the term is frequently used in this letter to refer to persons. We could also point to 14:37 as a parallel usage.

I would suggest that "men" and "gifts" are so closely linked in the thought of the Corinthians that the question addressed to Paul concerned both spiritual men and gifts. Perhaps the question could be restated as follows: "Don't the spiritual gifts prove that we are spiritual?" If, however, the question had been asked by those who were intimidated by the spirituals it might read: "Is it true that spiritual gifts are the sign of spiritual men?"

We can relate to this question. There probably aren't many pastors who have not been asked a question that resembles this in content. "Is it true that I must speak in tongues to be filled with the Spirit?" "Are we missing out on something here in our church?" Most laypersons have at some time been confronted by a well-meaning friend who has had what they consider to be a profound spiritual experience. They testify to it by pointing to an objective sign that proves that they have had a "valid" experience. This study may well help us to answer such questions.

Paul responded to this question with a term that summarized the Corinthian situation in a comprehensive fashion because he had to deal with "men" and "gifts" to properly address the needs of the total community. Paul wanted to develop a constructive and positive understanding of spiritual gifts within the whole body of believers. This entire three-chapter section can thus be understood as the answer to this simple question.

One final matter should be noted in the initial response. Paul's treatment of gifts/men was framed by terms which stress understanding. The statement "I do not want you to be unaware" may well have been intended to deflate the pride of the spirituals who boasted about their knowledge. Since gifts were central to the claim to spirituality, they must have believed themselves to be especially knowledgable about gifts. There was more than a tinge of irony in this statement. They believed they had an abundance of gifts and possessed all knowledge. Yet their arrogant behavior had demonstrated that they understood nothing about the true nature of spiritual gifts. However, the real significance of this statement is not made clear until we finish this section. Glance ahead to 1 Corinthians 14:37-38. Having completed his entire teaching, Paul declared that anyone who did not recognize the truth of his teaching would not be recognized. If the spirituals remained ignorant (same Greek word that is translated "unware" in 12:1) about the true nature of spiritual gifts after reading Paul's letter, they proved themselves not to be spiritual persons.

The Primary Corrective: Jesus is Lord

The reader is hardly prepared for Paul's first words in response to their question. Why did he appeal to their idolatrous past and then introduce the shocking phrase "Jesus is accursed"? It should not be overlooked that its placement here and the flow of the passage indicate that Paul intended this as a central part of his argument. Here clarity is gained by focusing on the whole, rather than the details. We must also continue to pay careful attention to the historical situation.

Since the possession of the Spirit *(pnuema)* and the resulting spiritual gifts *(pneumatika)* was at the heart of the Corinthian difficulties, Paul first focused attention on the work of the Spirit in all believers. Notice that there are 12 references to the Spirit in the first 13 verses of this chapter. This can only be fully appreciated when one understands that the Spirit is not mentioned in the two passages concerning spiritual gifts following 1 Corinthians. Verses 7 and 11 frame the first gift list and demonstrate the central purpose of the discussion. "But to *each* one is given the manifestation of the *Spirit* . . . But one and the *same* Spirit works all these things, distributing to *each one* individually just as He wills" (vv. 7, 11, author's italics). This point is made even more explicit by the fourfold repetition of *Spirit* in the gift list (vv. 8-10) in phrases such as "according to the same Spirit" and "by the one Spirit." This section is linked with the body imagery by the important reminder: "For by *one Spirit* we *all* were baptized into one body . . . and we *all* were made to drink of *one Spirit.*" (v. 13, author's italics). This common work of the Spirit is also the subject of verses 1-3, but it has largely gone unnoticed because of the overemphasis on the phrase "Jesus is accursed."

In fact, the first verses form the foundation upon which the corrective teaching on gifts and the spiritual person is built. Paul underlined an exceedingly elementary point, but one which had gone unnoticed in the Corinthian confusion. The confession "Jesus is Lord" cannot be made "except by the Holy Spirit." Paul thus countered the boasting of the spirituals by affirming that at the most fundamental level every believer is a spiritual person.

What then is the function of the blunt and unexpected "Jesus is accursed"? The difficulty of reconstructing a situation in which "Jesus is accursed" could have been uttered in a Christian gathering has led to a great number of creative suggestions such as: a curse uttered because of persecution, a Jewish curse, a curse uttered in a tongue, a Gnostic curse or a curse denying the resurrection. Others have simply stated that "Jesus is accursed" is nothing more than the hypothetical opposite of "Jesus is Lord." While this latter solution seems to be the easiest, some have objected that the very suggestion that anyone could curse Jesus under the inspiration of the Spirit is so utterly incomprehensible that its presence here is the height of foolishness. This objection is well made, for that is precisely the reaction that Paul intended to elicit. We might loosely paraphrase this verse: "It is *obvious* that a person could not curse Jesus when speaking in the Spirit; in the same manner it should be *clear* that every person who confesses that Jesus is Lord is a spiritual person!"

We have the popular equivalent of this today when someone declares something so obvious that it need not be said. You walk out of a building into a heavy rainstorm. Without thinking you spontaneously declare, "It's raining!" Almost certainly someone will respond; "Really, Sherlock?" There is a friendly barb which suggests that the evidence of the rain is so obvious to everyone it need not be mentioned. In the same manner, Paul used the obvious—*no one could curse Jesus speaking by the Spirit of God*—to dramatize an equally obvious truth—*no one can say Jesus is Lord except by the Spirit.* Thus Paul's first corrective was to refute the exclusivistic claim by the spirituals that they alone possessed the Spirit. Their claim, as we shall see, was based on the possession of certain spectacular gifts. Paul appealed to the most fundamental truth of the Christian experience—salvation through the work of the Spirit—to prove his point. Paul again underlined this truth in verse 13 of this chapter where he asserted: "For by one Spirit we were all baptized into one body."

In my pastoral duties I regularly encounter Christians who are experiencing doubts about the depth of their spiritual condition because someone has suggested that they do not have or are not baptized in the Spirit unless they speak in tongues or possess a certain gift. In like manner, I have met very sincere folks who have developed a spiritual arrogance because they had been taught that their possession of a certain gift proved they had something that others were missing. Out of genuine concern they had become self-styled evangelists for a certain gift or sign such as tongues. This belief leads to spiritually unhealthy conclusions on the part of both parties, and destroys the fellowship of the church. This danger existed in Corinth and exists today. Paul's words still stand—"No one can say 'Jesus is Lord' except by the Holy Spirit." Let's rejoice together since "by one Spirit we were all baptized into one body."

Verses 2 and 3 are bound together by a very strong Greek connective translated "therefore" (NASB). Paul was not interested in comparing pagan and Christian inspiration, nor was he giving a guide for the discerning of spirits as some commentators suggest. The last phrase of verse 2—"however you were led"—was a rather casual remark and demonstrated a lack of interest in pagan inspiration. Paul reminded the Corinthians of their pre-Christian existence for one purpose only. He wanted to clearly underline the work of the Spirit in their conversion experience. Before Paul could discuss gifts in a positive fashion, he had to first establish that every believer is a *spiritual person* in the most fundamental sense since the basic confession "Jesus is Lord" cannot be made except by the work of the Holy Spirit. Second, with this reference to the confession "Jesus is Lord," Paul brought the discussion of gifts within the perspective of the Lordship of Christ. It is only in this context of personal relationship with Christ and thus the common possession of the Spirit that Paul could put forward his corrective teaching on "gifts for ministry."

The Introduction of *Charisma*

Having thus established that the Spirit works in all persons in their conversion and thus all believers are "spirituals," Paul moved a step further to assure them that *all believers* possessed gifts for ministry (notice 12:6,7,11 and 14 *ff.*). The possession of gifts for ministry did not constitute, for Paul, an argument that a person is a spiritual person in a boastful sense. On the contrary, it demonstrated that all believers alike have received grace. Accordingly Paul replaced *pneumatika* (manifestation of the Spirit) with *charismata* (manifestation of grace). This replacement of terms is not obvious in most English translations but it has tremendous significance.

The Greek term *charismata* is the word from which we get charismatic. In most contexts where I hear it used today, the meaning we give to *charismatic* is actually what the Corinthians meant when they used *pneumatika*. Paul intentionally used *charismata* rather than *pneumatika* to introduce a much-needed corrective.

There are few extant uses of *charisma* prior to Paul, and this has led to a consensus among biblical scholars that Paul either coined this phrase or at least made it a specifically Christian term. We must ask why this particular term emerged with such force and consistency at this moment in history. It certainly cannot be argued that this was simply the first opportunity Paul had to use the term. Twice previously, Paul discussed community ministry (1 Thess. 5 and Gal. 6) but this term was not used.

It is important to notice that by substituting *charismata* for *pnuematika* Paul brought "gifts for ministry" under the corrective umbrella of *charis* (grace), a prominent theme of this letter. Don't misunderstand. Paul did not use *charismata* to divorce the gifts from the work of the Holy Spirit as verse 11 clearly demonstrates. Paul simply argued that the "gifts for ministry" are the result of God's grace in the life of every believer and therefore they offer no grounds for spiritual pride.

It is instructive to note that a similar corrective is found in 1 Corinthians 1:27-31, where Paul insisted that human boasting was excluded before God because God Himself is the very source of life. Notice also in chapter 2, Paul placed the wisdom of God against that of the spirituals. True spiritual persons have received the Spirit who is from God: "That we might know the things freely given [derivative of *charis*] to us by God" (2:12). This thought is also central to the argument of chapter 3. Paul insisted that he could not call them spiritual persons but babes because of their strife and zealousness to exalt one leader over another. Notice that the root cause of their strife is their lack of true spiritual wisdom. Otherwise they would have understood that Paul and Apollos were merely men, servants through whom God worked. Paul and Apollos had different ministries and opportunities, but God caused the growth (3:6). Paul laid the foundation but that in itself was "According to the grace *(charis)* of God which was given to me" (v. 10). As noted earlier, the corrective of 4:7 is essentially the same. "And what do you have that you did not receive?"

The most important corrective usage of *charisma* prior to 1 Corinthians 12:4 occurs in 1:4-7. *Charisma* appears for the first time in verse 7 and its meaning is defined by *charis*. Paul acknowledged their richness in speech and knowledge but indicated that their abundance had a direct correlation with their having received grace *(charismata)* in v. 4). The introduction of the term *charismata* in this opening paragraph foreshadows the discussion of spiritual gifts in chapters 12—14. Paul echoed their boast to abundance of gifts but insisted that these can only be properly evaluated when they are understood in the context of God's grace.

There is one other instance where Paul used the term *charisma* to curb arrogant boasting. In 1 Corinthians 7 Paul addressed numerous questions concerning marriage and singleness. Some Corinthians were apparently living a celibate life and were boasting about their celibacy. Paul approved of the life-style (7:7) but he insisted that the ability to live as a celibate cannot be grounds for boasting since it is also a gift of grace. Notice that here Paul used *charisma* in a way quite different from the usage in 1 Corinthians 12—14. Celibacy cannot be classified as a gift for ministry. This poses no real difficulty. *Charisma* was not a technical term that always had the same meaning. *Charisma* is used here to stop the arrogant boasting in one's life-style.

Variety Among the Pneumatika

Even the casual reader will notice the emphasis on variety. Some interpreters have attempted to divide the gifts into different categories based on the three words *gifts, ministries,* and *effects* (vv. 4-6). The linking of these terms with "Spirit," "Lord," and "God" respectively should warn against such arbitrary distinctions. All three terms view one matter—gifts for ministry—from different perspectives. *Gifts (charisma)* emphasize the graciousness of the Spirit in giving and thus excludes boasting. *Ministries (diakonia)* indicates that the manifestations of the Spirit cannot be regarded as spiritual privileges, but these are to be viewed as God-given means for service. Jesus' emphasis on the priority of service must have had a profound impact on Paul and the early disciples. Finally, *effects (energēma*) exalts God as the Source and energizer of all activities of service accomplished within the Christian community. There is a crescendo which draws attention to God as the *ultimate Source of all gifts.* This emphasis is given added attention by the reminder that it is the same God "who works all things in all persons" (v. 6).

The repetition of "variety" contrasted with the repetition of "same" (same Spirit . . . same Lord . . . same God) impressively lays the foundation for Paul's insistence that variety and unity are not opposites. They are both divinely given. The spirituals, by placing a premium on a few miraculous "sign" gifts, had been guilty of neglecting the diversity of gifts available to the Christian community.

Verse 7 serves as a bridge between verses 4-6 and 8-11, acting both as a summary and an introduction. Two points are made, with the emphasis on the second. First, Paul emphatically declared that each Christian, not just the "spiritually elite" was given a manifestation of the Spirit. Paul thus prepared the way for refuting the inflated claims of the spirituals on the basis of their own criterion—the possession of spiritual gifts. Second, no one was given a manifestation of the Spirit for personal gratification but for the common good. This was suggested by the use of ministries *(diakonia)* in verse 5, but it is stated here in unequivocal terms. Gifts are not given to a few for spiritual self-glorification but to each one for ministry. Both of these points will be illustrated through the body imagery and then restated more strongly and with new significance in the last half of this chapter.

Now we come to what has been of great interest to most Bible students—the first Pauline gift list (vv. 8-10). The repetition of "one" and "another" stressed that a variety of gifts were already claimed by different individuals in Corinth. While it is apparent that the list was not intended to be comprehensive, the gifts here were not chosen haphazardly. The list as a whole deserves close attention. Several important characteristics emerge.

1. These gifts would have been prominent in the gathered assembly.

2. They are the gifts most frequently referred to by people today as "miraculous."

3. A majority of the gifts are directly related to speech and revelation.

4. It follows that there is little continuity between these gifts and any permanent abilities possessed before one becomes a Christian.

5. Many of these gifts could well be described as momentary expressions of the Spirit.

Why would Paul include such a miraculous list at this point? The Corinthian letter as a whole seems to indicate that a part of the dilemma is that not all the believers at Corinth possessed such miraculous expressions of the Spirit as we find listed here. Nevertheless, this list follows Paul's strong assertion that each one possessed a manifestation of the Spirit for the common good. It almost appears that Paul has virtually retreated from his earlier position and agreed with their emphasis on a few miraculous gifts.

The gifts mentioned in this list are, in fact, an accurate representation of the "spiritual manifestation" *(pneumatika)* which were eagerly sought by the spirituals because of their sign value. They were visible and dramatic, easy to display in the worship service, and thus provided ready proof that these folks already reigned. A glance at 1:5-7 and 13:1-3 will demonstrate the exaggerated interest in a few sign gifts. The listing of such miraculous gifts at this point may at first appear to be a concession to the spirituals. In truth, it was an important plank in Paul's argument. The impressiveness of such miraculous manifestations would have made the claims of the spirituals convincing. Their possession by the spirituals, no doubt, had caused doubts and confusion in the minds of those lacking such gifts. We see a clear parallel in much of modern-day Christianity when a few gifts are claimed for sign value and so-called nongifted believers are caused to wonder if they have missed something.

I am not suggesting that the spirituals had drawn up a list such as this. They viewed these manifestations in a rather monolithic fashion, as miraculous signs, and had not really observed that even these gifts were in fact quite diverse. Paul therefore utilized the manifestations valued by the spirituals to establish that a variety of gifts was already present in Corinth. Having established this principle of variety with their chosen gifts, he later would expand the scope of his argument to include functions not previously considered by the spirituals. Second, by listing these manifestations, Paul demonstrated that he did not oppose their "miraculous" manifestations. He acknowledged them as the work of the Spirit, and as such they were given for the common good. They must now be used in such a manner as to edify the body.

You should notice that in verse 11 Paul stated that the same Spirit has empowered all these gifts "distributing to each one individually just as He wills." There was no contradiction for Paul to say that God (v. 6) and the Spirit (v. 11) energize the gifts. Paul agreed that the Spirit energizes all these abilities for service, but he stressed that the Spirit apportions to each as *He* wills. The emphasis falls on the sovereignty of the Giver and reminds us that the possession of any one of these gifts cannot be used as an argument that one individual is more spiritual than another. Thus far in the treatment of the gifts, Paul had intentionally used gifts claimed by the spirituals to establish his corrective points. It is, of course, sound argumentation and good pastoral procedure to make a point of correction using agreed upon material. Paul did this to establish a base from which he could broaden the entire understanding of gifts for ministry.

A point of interest should be pointed out for your continued observation. A significant fact that is often overlooked is that the Spirit will not be mentioned again in connection with the "gifts." In Romans the Giver is God and in Ephesians the Giver is the ascended Lord. This observation coupled with the fact that Paul inserted *charismata* (v. 4) (manifestation of grace) as he answered their question on *pnuematika* (v. 1) (manifestation of the Spirit) should not be ignored. Paul was trying to correct the spiritual arrogance that had developed on the basis of sign gifts. In Romans and Ephesians it is likely that Paul was anxious to avoid in those communities the spiritual misunderstanding that had developed in Corinth. For that reason he avoided discussing "gifts" and Spirit in the same context. The very title of this book was used to accomodate the popular misunderstanding about gifts. We would have been more accurate to entitle it *Grace Gifts: Empowering the New Testament Church,* but that might not have been understandable to many persons.

The Body Imagery

The human body is a pretty miraculous instrument, particularly when all parts are working in order. Yet when one part fails to perform properly for any reason, the whole body is affected. Most of us remember the most common pain of childhood—stumping our big toe. Can you recall the pain that shot through the body when you drove your toe into the raised section of the sidewalk? But you continued on your way thinking, *Well it's only one toe.* You limped on down the street but soon began to notice that your thigh and hip had started to throb with pain because of your awkward gait. The pain crawled up your spine and soon you hurt all over. Big toes are usually neglected until they fail to function properly. Then we realize the value of this small part to the rest of the body. Paul drew attention to the human body to illustrate both the need for variety and mutual care. For our churches to work properly, all the body parts must work in harmony and empathy. This imagery will not only help us to understand the correctives needed in Corinth, but also those needed in our churches today.

In this section Paul moved his argument a step further by means of the extended metaphor of the body. This section is somewhat difficult to follow because Paul utilized the imagery for several distinct purposes. This imagery was not intended primarily to illustrate points not yet clear, but was the means whereby Paul could introduce a more expansive understanding of gifts for ministry.

Paul first called attention to the makeup of the physical body. The point emphasized by repetition is that *all* the members of the human body, whatever their differences, belong to the *one body*. The human body clearly illustrates that unity and diversity are a divine necessity for the proper functioning of the body. The conclusion, "so also is Christ," (v. 12) is abrupt, because it was intended to direct the reader's attention from the human illustration to the spiritual truth concerning the Christian community. Paul actually took two steps at once in this conclusion. He could have said, "So also is the church," but he more pointedly concluded "So also is Christ," because the church is the body of Christ.

In verse 13 Paul continued the emphasis on the work of the Spirit which all believers share alike. This is, however, the final reference to the Spirit in this chapter, and it is the pivotal point which enabled Paul to move his gift teaching beyond the limited understanding of the spirituals. Recall with me the fact that Paul previously underlined the work of the Spirit in the life of the individual believer. The Spirit enabled every believer to confess "Jesus is Lord," and He dispensed the gifts to each as He willed. Paul was careful, almost pedantically so, to stress that one and the same Spirit has accomplished these things in the life of the individual believer.

In verse 13 he took the next logical step by emphasizing that the *one Spirit* had brought *all believers* in Corinth into a *single body*. The stress is clearly on the corporate work of the Spirit who creates unity by incorporating the many believers into one body. This emphasis is wholly consistent with Paul's insistence that although the manifestations were given to *each* believer, they were intended for the good of the body. It was necessary first to use truths even the spirituals could accept, in order to move them to an understanding of the role of the gifts in the life of the community. Paul first affirmed the individual's participation in the Spirit (echoing the emphasis of the spirituals) in order to share a more important but woefully neglected truth. The *one Spirit* incorporates all true believers in *one body*. It was an important corrective to place the gifts in the total context of the life of the community. The spirituals had clamored for them only in an individualistic fashion as a sign of spiritual achievement.

The uniqueness of Christian unity which yet preserves individuality is well illustrated by Paul's reference to various national and social groups represented in the Christian community. "Jews or Greeks . . . slaves or free," all were baptized into one body and all were made to drink of one Spirit. The reference to a common experience of water baptism (see Eph. 4:5) was not simply a nostalgic reminder of a past event, but was intended to impress upon the Corinthians, as vividly as possible, the corporate and unifying work of the Spirit. By the intense spiritual individualism, the Corinthians were threatening to destroy the very unity the Spirit desired to create. Ironically, by the zeal to possess only the *pneumatika* (more miraculous gifts), they had ignored the God-given variety necessary for unity and thus were hurting the body.

By arguing that the one Spirit who gives the gifts creates the body, Paul was able to bring the gifts under the corrective which permeates this letter—the concern of the true spiritual person for fellow Christians (see esp. 8:12-13; 10:23-33; 11:29,33). To establish this point firmly, Paul turned to an extended illustration based on the working of the human body. Paul's use of a familiar analogy was striking, with the examples often verging on the ridiculous.

"For the body is not one member, but many" sets the tone of the passage and shows that throughout Paul was concerned about the individualistic view of the spirituals. The foot and the ear are first pictured as arguing that they are not a part of the body because they are not the hand or eye. We may consider our foot to be less glamourous than our hand or our ear to be less vital than our eye. But in truth all the parts are vital. They are different because the unity of the body requires diversity in function. When one considers the human body, the claim is clearly nonsensical. The zeal of the spirituals to be alike in possessing the miraculous gifts had resulted in a failure to appreciate the diversity of the body and in turn led to rampant individualism which caused them to act without consideration of other believers. Paul suggested that the behavior of the spirituals had been tantamount to saying that the ear or foot were not even members of the body. Thus the point is made: all members, whatever their function, belong to the one body.

It is frequently easy to smile at the mistakes of those in the past without seeing our similar failings. Anytime we hear the suggestion that I'm more gifted or valuable to the church than another person because of my abilities or position, we make the same mistake as the spirituals. Sometimes we pastors are chief offenders as we chase after the multitalented people in our community, our only thought being how valuable they will be to the life of the church. Sometimes we may even be led to neglect that person who may not appear to be very gifted or useful to the needs of the fellowship. Or conversely, I frequently hear someone suggest that they are of no value to the church because of their assumed lack of ability for ministry. Apparently they are thinking, "I can't preach, teach, or sing and therefore I am unimportant." But with Paul we must retort, "It is not for this reason any the less a part of the body" (v. 15).

In verses 17-19 Paul posed three separate questions which frame the central thought concerning God's sovereign design of the body (v. 18). If we were to string the questions together they would sound like this: "If all the body were an eye . . . If all the body were an ear . . . If they were all one part. . .?" All three questions point out the necessity of diversity. Equality of function would, in fact, destroy the body (v. 19), a danger which was all too real in Corinth. The central verse of this passage is verse 18. The denial of diversity, either in theory or practice, not only has practical consequences, but it contradicts the very will of God. He has constructed the body just as He desired. The emphatic "each one of them" actually interupts the flow of the sentence and could hardly be more pointed. The human body has numerous members, precisely because there is a variety of functions which must take place for the body to exist. Consequently, there is a natural interdependence among the body's members.

I am always amused when I hear folks talk about their independence, whether they are talking about themselves or their church. We usually say, "I don't need anybody else to be a Christian, I can serve the Lord on my own." This whole line of thinking is reflected in this very passage. We are not independent, we are interdependent. We need one another to function. God has so designed the spiritual body that we must be fully dependent on one another. Since no one can possess all the gifts, we are all in need of others. "And the eye cannot say to the hand, 'I have no need of you.'" (v. 24). The head might determine that the body should move, but without the feet to respond there would be no movement. Thus, just in terms of function we are dependent in two ways. Whatever my specific gifts, I depend upon other gifted members to minister to my spiritual needs. Secondly, any gift isolated from the full ministry of the body will have no effect. Thus each one of us depends upon other gifts to give meaning to our gifts.

Who Are the Unseemly?

The body metaphor is pressed even further with the Corinthian situation still in mind. The spirituals were saying, either verbally or by their actions, that they had no need for other Christians, particularly those who were weaker and without honor. The spirituals believed they had been especially honored by God. The inferior members were of no use; in fact they were a hindrance. What could an ordinary believer possibly contribute to one who already reigns? In order to fully understand this section we must realize that "weaker," "unseemly," and "less honorable" do not simply refer to eyes, internal organs, or genitalia as most commentators suggest; they refer to the other members in Corinth as viewed by the spirituals. This may actually reflect terminology used by the spirituals. It is instructive to look at several passages in 1 Corinthians where similar terms are found. In 1:26 *ff,* Paul reminded the Corinthians that, when they were saved, not many of them were wise, mighty, or noble. This suggests that there were some who now clearly believed they were wise, mighty, and noble in a spiritual sense. The corrective of 1:26 *ff.* is similar to that of 12:21 *ff.* The priority is actually given to that which by human standards seems humble and undistinguished. God has chosen the foolish to shame the wise, and the weak to shame the strong, and the things which are not to nullify the things that are.

A more important passage is 4:8-13. The possession of the *pneumatika* had not only made the spirituals feel superior to their fellow Christians, but even to the apostles. The spirituals were already filled; they were rich and they were kings. In contrast the apostles were last of all, like men condemned to death. They were a spectacle to the world. Verse 10 deserves citing in full: "We are *fools* for Christ's sake, but ye are wise in Christ; we are *weak,* but ye are strong; ye are honorable, but we are *despised*" (KJV, author's italics). One doesn't have to read too closely to hear the ironic edge to that verse.

The same type of irony is present in 12:21-26. Although the spirituals thought they were most important and that they were especially honored by God, the very opposite was true. The weaker parts (by their standards) were indispensable. Those parts which are deemed less honorable by human standards are invested with greater honor and the parts we think to be unrepresentable are treated with greater modesty. This passage is strongly polemical. Paul actually rejected the spirituals' criteria for evaluating which manifestations of the Spirit are most honorable. They had chosen those most visible for selfish reasons. Spiritual gifts are for the common good so we should desire those which are of greater service to the body (14:12). The arrogance of the spirituals was attacked as well as their attitude toward those whom they had deemed to be less honorable because they lacked miraculous gifts.

Could it be that Paul had in mind the popular teaching of Jesus in which the order of popular evaluation was radically reversed (see Mark 10:35-45)? For Jesus the servant, the one deemed to be lowest, was in fact the highest. Those desiring greatness must choose to become servants. In any case, Paul clearly echoed the preference for service over personal exaltation. Paul verified this reversal of values by stating that God Himself has "composed" or blended together the body in this way. We would do well to examine our own thinking on this matter. Do we truly believe that servanthood is the highest form of service? Do you find folks lining up in your church for the unheralded areas of service? Do you have a waiting list to work in preschool? How many folks are standing in line to serve on the clean-up detail after the church picnic? Could it be that we have been infected with the disease of the spirituals in our preference for the more visible and more honorable areas of ministry?

Don't misunderstand. Paul's aim was not to discredit the *pneumatika,* but to help the immature spirituals to understand the role of God's sovereign grace in the granting of all gifts. Further, Paul wanted to relate them properly to the community. He wanted them to evaluate their desire for particular gifts based on the need of the body rather than their own ego gratification. The dilemma of the spirituals is echoed in the popular phrase: "They were so heavenly minded, they were no earthly good." Gifts for them were signs of their heavenly status, not gifts of grace equipping them to minister.

Encouraging Mutual Care

Since God has created the body to be interdependent, there must be no discord. The word is *schism* (schisma), as in 1:10 and 11:18. We have already seen that schism did exist in Corinth. Discord in the church is not just wrong, it is disasterous because it inhibits the proper working of the body. Could you imagine the result if your brain and mouth were in discord? Possibly, you have had that to happen. It can cause great harm to your physical well-being. In like manner discord in the body of Christ keeps it from effective service. The mission of the church is too important for us to allow discord to creep in and drain away our power.

In the place of discord there should be mutual care (v. 25b) and empathy (v. 26b). We have already seen several examples where mutual care was lacking in Corinth. The Christians, who through their knowledge had determined that idol meat was acceptable, had not considered the effect their eating might have on a weaker brother. The Corinthian celebration of the Lord's Supper was a prime example where mutual care was lacking. Thus Paul had taken the theme of interdependence one step further. As members of the same body we are so closely bound together that we actually share the same feelings. What causes joy for one member, delights the body. When one member suffers, the entire body hurts. When we begin to embrace the theology of gifts to this point in our churches, we will experience the empowering of God through the gifts.

Paul pressed home the entire body imagery in an unmistakeable fashion: "Now you are Christ's body, and individually members of it" (v. 27). Paul's primary focus was to remind the spirituals that they were members of the fellowship at Corinth and thus they were integrally linked to all other members. Nevertheless, there was also an implicit linking of the individualistic Corinthians to the larger Christian community. The reminder that they were individually related to the body indicated that they were not simply absorbed into the body losing their personal identity, but that each respectively, by the grace of God, had a distinctive place and function. Paul could now make this point because he had shown that all believers participate in the one Spirit who incorporates them into one body, and who has given each a charismatic (gracious) endowment that each might fulfill a unique function for the good of the whole. A proper understanding of spiritual gifts is one of the most affirming and challenging of all biblical doctrines. You are important to the proper functioning of your church! Are you serving according to your gift?

A Second Gift List

It should be noted that Paul had not yet made it entirely clear, particularly to the spirituals, how he could say that all are gifted. It is true that he had argued that all participate in the one Spirit who gives gifts as He wills, but the fact still remained that some in Corinth had not shown any evidence of possessing the gifts mentioned in

12:8-10. It is for this reason that Paul included a second listing of gifts which differs in several ways from the first.

The passage begins with the note that God Himself has placed (see v. 28) in the church apostles, prophets, and so forth. The idea of the body was thus continued with a particular emphasis on God's organization of the Christian body. It is unwise to read too much into the order of the entire list. Nevertheless, the obvious numerical ordering of the first three entries plus the use of individuals, as opposed to abilities thereafter, was certainly intended to draw the reader's attention to the apostles, prophets, and teachers. The listing of individuals almost certainly would have caused the Corinthians to think concretely of persons with whom they were acquainted who were carrying out these functions. The apostles, prophets, and teachers were involved in leadership functions from the very beginning of the Christian community. They participated in the work of proclamation and clarification of the Gospel.

The spirituals were aware of the presence of such individuals in Corinth, and many of the difficulties can be traced to the spirituals' willingness to criticize leaders and to press for their own rights. Paul's apostolic authority had little meaning to the spirituals. They judged a man by his commanding presence and spiritual manifestations (1 Cor. 2:2-3; 4:6-13; and see 2 Cor. 10:10 to 12:13, esp. 10:10).

First Corinthians 16:15-16 suggests that there were persons, notably the household of Stephanas, who had emerged as the leaders of the Corinthian congregation, but they had been ignored by the spirituals. Paul emphasized that God organized the body in order to provide for its unity. With particular emphasis on apostles, prophets, and teachers, Paul quite clearly was saying that there is a leadership structure which has been established in the church by God (see Eph. 4:11). To fail to recognize the work of these individuals is the same as ignoring the will of God (see on 14:37 *ff.*).

A second point can be made. By bringing the apostles, prophets, and teachers into close juxtaposition with manifestations such as gifts of healing and tongues, Paul was pointing out, much to the surprise of the spirituals, that these men were also charismatic. The breadth of the Pauline concept of *charisma* is becoming apparent. The "official" leaders of the communities had been gifted by God for leadership. The abilities enabling them to function as leaders were no less miraculous and no less "spiritual" than those abilities being displayed by the *pneumatikoi.*

Yet Paul broadened further the "accepted" understanding of "spiritual manifestations." He now listed two unusual gifts—"helps" and "administrations." It is unimportant that Paul never again used either of these terms in a listing of gifts. Paul intended to demonstrate that even quite "mundane" abilities such as those enabling one to administrate or do helpful tasks are also *charismata.* These remind us of the person who declares they can't lead or teach but they'll be glad to keep records, serve on a committee, or do parking lot duty. Good news! These are also gifts from God for service and are just as supernatural as any other gift for ministry. Possibly these functions should be closely related to those who were deemed to be "unseemly" or "weaker," but in any case the two terms introduce an entirely new area of gifts for ministry.

It is interesting that both leadership abilities and these "mundane" service abilities are more permanent in nature and also more closely related to the abilities one might possess before conversion than those of 12:8-10. Paul made no distinction between extraordinary and ordinary abilities, or between transitory or permanent manifestations—all alike are *charismata.*

We have now looked at two Pauline gift lists in this one chapter. The first enumerated only the prized gifts of the spirituals. Paul wanted them to see the diversity in their own gifts. In the second list Paul literally pulled the top and the bottom out of the list and thus expanded the accepted definition of spiritual gifts. He expanded upon the miraculous by adding leadership abilities and service abilities. Neither list was intended to be comprehensive, nor do we gain anything by trying to add up the two lists and calculate the specific number of gifts available to the church. These lists were merely teaching tools.

The rhetorical questions of verses 29-30 echo the truth established in verses 17-19 about the natural body. They anticipate a negative reply and thus show the necessity of diversity. Paul repeated the list of 12:28 in the same order but excluded helps and administration. Some scholars suggest they were left out because they were non-charismatic and therefore could be done by anyone. That, however, contradicts the point made by their inclusion in 12:28. Could it be that their exclusion was intended to actually draw attention to them? It is obvious that all do not have leadership roles or possess "miraculous" gifts. However, in light of Paul's broader definition it should now be apparent that all have some gift for ministry although it might appear quite mundane.

Desire the Greater Gifts

Verse 31 provides the transition leading to the central discussion of chapter 13. It is probable that the phrase "earnestly desire the greater gifts" *(zēloō)* was a conspicuous allusion to the zeal of the spirituals for the *pneumatika* (miraculous gifts) and may in fact echo a slogan of the spirituals. Here as in 14:1, 12, and 39 the "zeal for gifts" is immediately qualified by the phrase that follows it. Paul appealed to their zeal in order to encourage them to be zealous for the greater gifts. What is meant by "greater gifts"? Some scholars argue that it refers to the ecstatic or miraculous gifts. That would accurately portray the spirituals' evaluation, but Paul intended this as a corrective, and consequently he employed his preferred term, *charismata.* Therefore, we must ask what Paul desired to convey with this positive redirection of their zeal.

It is possible to understand greater *charismata* in terms of the broadened scope of Paul's listing of gifts as contrasted with the spirituals' narrow concept of the *pnuematika.* Thus Paul would be encouraging them to be zealous for the whole scope of charismatic abilities, including leadership and service abilities as illustrated in the preceding discussion and list. However, it is more probable, given the full context of chapters 12—14, that by greater *charismata* Paul meant those *charismata* which were better suited for edifying the church. This point will be made explicit in chapter 14, but the way has already been paved by the emphasis on the common good in 12:7 and the reversal of values in 12:21 *ff.* While all gifts are expressions of God's grace and all are necessary for the proper functioning of the body, some gifts are more valuable in terms of their contribution to the edification of the church. We will see this clearly in the interpretation of chapter 14. Paul's evaluation of greater gifts involved edification of the body and not miraculous sign value.

The phrase "I show you a still more excellent way," introduces another dimension to the discussion of the Corinthian problem of spiritual gifts. The reader should be cautious not to read too much into this one phrase. Paul was not suggesting that love was a better way to gain the gifts. In like manner he was not contrasting love with the gifts as if the Corinthians should seek love instead of the gifts. The attributes of love are not the "greater gifts." Spiritual gifts are essential to the life of the church and thus cannot be put aside even for love.

You will also notice that several of the gifts are listed in 13:1-3 in a context that is slightly negative in which they are contrasted with love. This should not cause the reader to assume that Paul had a negative evaluation of these actual gifts. They are used by way of example to set the stage for a much-needed corrective teaching. As we have already noticed, Paul gave the spiritual gifts the highest possible evaluation by calling them *charismata* and by relating them to the body of Christ. Now Paul wanted to place the grace gifts into their proper perspective in the life of the community by placing them in an even larger context. There is a way to determine true spirituality! It is a way beyond their present calculations—the way of love.

4
The Spiritual Man Redefined

"Pastor, we've got great news. We're getting married and we want you to do the service. Just do anything you like in the wedding. We have one request. We want you to read the beautiful hymn about love."

"Do you mean Paul's discussion of love in 1 Corinthians 13?"

"Yeah that's the one! Isn't it the most beautiful thing you've ever read."

I can't tell you how many times I've heard this request. There's nothing wrong with desiring to have 1 Corinthians 13 in one's wedding. I usually incorporate it into my ceremonies. It is beautiful and it does describe love in a profound way. But our familiarity with it as a "hymn about love" can cause us to miss its centrality to Paul's teaching on spiritual gifts. Scholars have, for the same reasons, often failed to understand its full impact on a discussion of gifts.

Paul's Word of Wisdom

Scholars have long been impressed by the beauty, style, and depth of the teaching of 1 Corinthians 13. This has led some to call it a "hymn" and to assign it to someone other than Paul, and others have suggested that it was composed by Paul on a separate occasion. In this light it becomes a polished gem inserted here because of its relevance to the present discussion. Yet some find its insertion at this point unfortunate and would place it next to chapter 8 or after chapter 14. These suggestions fail to appreciate the polemical tone of this section, and its centrality for Paul's corrective teaching. Its location between the broadened explanation of gifts for ministry (ch. 12) and the practical use of such gifts (ch. 14) is hardly accidental. Spiritual manifestations were at the heart of the Corinthian difficulties, and it is in the midst of this discussion that we discover the peak of Paul's corrective teaching.

Nevertheless, even a casual reading of this chapter will alert one to the fact that its style and content are different from its immediate context. Some commentators have been impressed by the fact that we find a similar style of writing in other wisdom literature of this same period. Why, we should ask, would Paul somewhat change gears in terms of style right in the middle of the discussion of gifts? It is likely that Paul intentionally chose this style of wisdom presentation at this high point in his argument to meet the spirituals on their own ground. You will recall that they loved to boast concerning their wisdom. Now Paul displayed wisdom teaching of his own. A similar situation can be found in 2 Corinthians 10—13 where Paul followed his opponents in boasting, but then reversed the tables by boasting of his weakness. Paul had been reproached by the spirituals because his preaching lacked persuasive words of wisdom. Ironically, Paul used "persuasive words of wisdom" to express his most pointed correction. Could a passage such as this have elicited the remark of 2 Corinthians 10:10? "His letters are weighty and strong, but his personal presence is unimpressive, and his speech contemptible."

Love, the Sign of Spiritual Maturity

But why did Paul move his argument to a higher level, virtually interrupting his discussion of gifts? The answer is in the unique relationship between spiritual gifts *(pneumatika)* and the spiritual persons *(pneumatikos)*. First Corinthians 13 is primarily about "persons" and only secondarily about gifts. Paul thus offered a comprehensive redefinition of the spiritual person. Love is in a sense contrasted with gifts, but this is due only to the exaggerated significance given to the gifts as the sign of the spiritual person. The first three verses demonstrate that Paul was concerned with the worth of persons and not just gifts themselves. Lest I be misunderstood, it is not that Paul was placing love against gifts and making love the "way" which renders gifts unimportant, nor was he describing the "way" which all must walk, whether gifted or not—for *all are gifted.*

Paul Turned the Tables

You will recall that the spirituals wanted miraculous signs to prove that they already reigned. Paul would establish that love is the one experience of eternal reality available in the present. Love is the *sign* that one is an authentic spiritual person. Love is not a gift and thus not the greatest gift. Love is relational; it finds its authenticity in the reality of God's love (Eph. 2:4-5). But God's love is experienced in the cross and therefore in the relationship the believer has with God in Jesus Christ. Love then becomes the controlling motive of Christian activity (1 Cor. 16:14; 2 Cor. 5:14): The Christian is called to walk in love (see Rom. 14:15). However, the activity of love is not the expression of human will but of the power of the Spirit through whom love is poured out in the believer's heart (see Rom. 5:5). Love, experienced in relationship with God, will be visible and controlling in the true spiritual person's relations with others. It is this practical, visible expression of love which Paul emphasized against the egotistical individualism of the spirituals. Love will be the controlling factor in the authentic spiritual person's desire for and use of spiritual gifts. The redefinition of the spiritual person will be taken up and applied in a pragmatic fashion in chapter 14 with a powerful conclusion (14:37 *ff.*).

Paul, in the first verses, depicted love as that which makes Christian existence truly Christian. Paul's corrective is given powerful impact by a comparison with the vaunted "sign-gifts" of the spirituals. Don't overlook the fact that these are the same gifts that have been a priority issue since chapter 1. There can be little doubt that tongue speaking held a prominent, though not exclusive, place as a sign of one's present reign in the Kingdom. The mysterious nature of such a gift commanded much attention. The extensive treatment of this gift in chapter 14 suggests both its importance and abuse in Corinth. This gift still seems to be at the heart of much of the confusion over spiritual gifts. So we will find this section relevant for evaluating present-day concerns.

The phrase "If I speak with the tongues of men and angels" has proved troublesome to most commentators. The majority have argued that it is symbolic for every possible type of speech in heaven and on earth. This is partially correct, but this passage is too pointed to allow one to accept this interpretation uncritically. Some who have difficulty with this view suggest that Paul believed glossolalia[1] to be the language of angels. But is there any support for such a contention? First Corinthians 14:2 cannot be claimed as proof. The main point of that verse is simply that human beings cannot understand glossolalia. Second Corinthians 12:4 is a more pertinent passage. Notice however that what Paul heard was "inexpressible words, which a man is not permitted to speak." Since the revelation in the vision could not be uttered, it cannot be glossolalia since that gift assumes speech. Further, we should note that Paul stated that tongues would cease when the perfect comes (13:10). If "perfect" referred to the fulness of God's kingdom in heaven, why would tongues cease just when they would prove to be particularly useful? Thus it is difficult to imagine that Paul considered this to be the language of heaven.

It is reasonable to suspect that the spirituals had claimed that their tongue speech was angelic speech. What clearer evidence could there be that one already reigned? Since Paul would not agree with that conclusion, 2 Corinthians 12:4 might have a slight barb to it. Man is neither able nor permitted to speak what he hears in paradise.

Paul's corrective was sharp. He used himself ("If I") to present a hypothetical case reflecting the claims of the spirituals. Thus Paul noted that one could speak with tongues of men and angels and yet be no more than an abrasive noise if he lacks love. Notice that the individual himself becomes like the noisy gong or clanging cymbal. Paul was not concerned at this point with the edifying value of any gift, but he was simply describing the effect of the individual who lacked love. "Noisy" and "clanging" may allude to pagan worship, and if that be the case, Paul's corrective was even more sharply defined. Tongues practiced by a person lacking love are much the same as the clanging of pagan worship. The main point of the discussion is clear: tongues do not prove that an individual is spiritual. Without love, the greatest tongues speaker is only a discordant sound.

"Prophecy," "mysteries," and "knowledge" are intricately related. They all demand "specific revelation" to function. The fine distinctions between the various speech and revelational gifts here and in 12:8-10 are difficult for us to reconstruct. It is possible that Paul had in mind some distinctions (see 14:6), but it is likely that the spirituals' boasts are most clearly reflected in the phrase "in all speech and in all knowledge" (1:5), and that subtle distinctions were irrelevant to them. The reader's attention is again drawn to the emphasis on abundance with the fourfold repetition of *all.* They knew all mysteries, had all knowledge and all faith. It has already been demonstrated that speech and revelational gifts were at the heart of the controversy in Corinth.

Further we noted that a number of the ethical difficulties could be specifically related to the spirituals' claim to possess special knowledge. The most striking example occurs in chapter 8. The spirituals had freely partaken of the idol meat on the basis of their knowledge (8:1,4). Paul did not refute their claim to knowledge. He simply contrasted the results of their knowledge which was arrogance (v. 1) and a stumbling block (v. 9) with the outcome of love which would be edification. Secondly, he indicated that their knowledge was not as full and mature as they liked to believe (8:2), a point which will be clarified in 13:12.

Miracle-working faith is next in this listing of gifts, and it is also present in 12:8-10. Although we have no discussion of miraculous deeds, as such, in 1 Corinthians, it is entirely conceivable that some had offered miraculous deeds as evidence of their spiritual status. There is a reference to miraculous acts in 2 Corinthians 12:12. While this verse is certainly relevant, it can only be used with some caution because the difficulties pictured in 2 Corinthians 10—13 clearly reflect the presence of new teachers who had come to Corinth since the writing of 1 Corinthians. Nevertheless, it seems that some of the Corinthians, possibly the unrepentant spirituals, had been impressed by the "most eminent apostles" (2 Cor. 11:5) who possessed miraculous abilities. In 2 Corinthians 10—13 Paul reluctantly entered their game of boasting, but first he turned the tables by boasting about his hardships. Finally, in 2 Corinthians 12 Paul did boast in an area similar to that in which his opponents had boasted. With some hesitancy he called attention to the fact that the signs of a true apostle had been performed among them.

The Acts account makes abundantly clear that "signs and wonders" regularly accompanied the ministry of the apostles (Acts 2:43; 4:30-31; 5:12; 6:8; 14:3; 15:12). Interestingly, Paul appeared to emphasize the "sign" of conversion. Notice for example the discussion in Romans 15:19 where Paul mentioned the signs and wonders and followed it with his emphasis on preaching the gospel. Many of the difficulties in Corinth were caused by the fascination by the immature Corinthians with miraculous "signs." Perhaps we can suggest that many of the community problems in Corinth could be understood in terms of their childish attempt to regularize and congregationalize that which God intended as a sign for the establishment of the New Testament church in the ministry of the apostles. In any case we know that the immature Corinthians were impressed by miraculous deeds, and thus we might suspect that even by the time of the writing of 1 Corinthians some were boasting to exercise such abilities.

It has often been noted that "faith, so as to remove mountains" echoed a saying of the Lord (Mark 11:23; Matthew 17:20, 21:21). It could be that the Corinthians were misusing sayings of the Lord to defend their insistence on "signs."[2] Thus again Paul simply reproduced the boast of the spirituals only to counter it. Paul's judgment was pointed. I may possess all these gifts in the greatest measure, but if I lack love, "I am nothing."

Verse 3 presents several difficulties: (1) there is nothing in 1 Corinthians to suggest the Corinthians were concerned about feeding the poor, and (2) there is a textual variant among early manuscripts. You will notice in numerous translations that there will be a footnote mentioning that some early manuscripts read "that I may boast." This would be in place of the phrase "to be burned." It is not an easy decision because the arrogant attitude of the Corinthians may seem to have favored the reading "that I may boast," but the reading "to be burned" is favored by the best manuscripts. Both of these difficulties are somewhat resolved when we remember the total context. In verses 1-3 Paul was taking some of the spirituals' most prized gifts and placing them in the most positive context possible. In this instance, Paul was not concerned about sacrificial self-giving, but was actually alluding to the spirituals' disregard for their physical body. Their disregard was not being expressed positively but arrogantly in numerous ways, sexual asceticism (ch. 7) and incest (ch. 5) being two. Thus even though the spirituals' disregard for the physical body had led to arrogant and destructive behavior; Paul, took the most positive expression of disregard for bodily existence ("give all my possessions to feed the poor"). Even such a noble act, devoid of love, would be of no benefit. This would make the contrast with the selfish Corinthians even more vivid. We might paraphrase this as follows, "You disregard the physical body for selfish reasons such as sexual indulgence and you're proud of that. Even if I were to disregard my body for the most noble reason possible, to benefit others, and I lack love, it is no spiritual benefit to me."

Love Versus the Behavior of the Spirituals

The startling statements of these first three verses would cause anyone to wonder, *What do you mean by love?* Paul was aware that it was altogether possible that the spirituals would miss the corrective nature of verses 1-3. He also knew that they might glibly think that they already excelled in loving behavior. Therefore Paul described in detail the behavior which would and would not emerge from love *(agape)*. Many commentaries note that love is shown to be the opposite of the natural man. While that is certainly true, the more significant point is that love was contrasted with the actual behavior of the spirituals. The eight negative statements were carefully selected to demonstrate conclusively that the spirituals lack love—the one true sign of spiritual maturity.

The first two positive statements in verse 4 are introductory and therefore somewhat general statements about the nature of love (see Gal. 5:22). Patient and kind emphasize one's behavior in relation to others. Patience is particularly important to the proper functioning of the Christian community (1 Thess. 5:14; Eph. 4:2). Love which is patient and kind will not be jealous *(zēloō)*. This is the same Greek word that we looked at early in our description of the spirituals. Spiritual zeal is laudable, but often in the Corinthian correspondence one discovers negative overtones (notice in 2 Cor. 11:2, Paul qualified his zeal as "Godly zeal"). The Corinthian zeal had degenerated into jealousy and self-striving. Their zeal for various wise leaders had demonstrated that they were in reality babes and not spirituals. They were zealous to possess the spiritual gifts (12:31; 14:1-2), but for all the wrong reasons. Zeal, untamed by love, exhibits itself in self-seeking jealousy. Love does not behave this way.

"Love does not brag and is not arrogant" but even a cursory reading of 1 Corinthians reveals that Paul constantly rebuked the spirituals for their arrogance and boasting (see 5:6). The Greek word translated "brag" is found only here in the New Testament. It suggests the picture of a windbag or in our jargon: "one who is swelled up like a toad." There was a bit of sarcasm intended. "Is not arrogant" was a particularly pointed condemnation of the spirituals, since this same word was used frequently by Paul to characterize the spirituals (see 4:6 *ff.;* 18 *ff.;* 5:2 *ff.;* 8:1 *ff.*). The spirituals had become inflated and had boasted concerning their wisdom and oratorical ability (1:5). They boasted concerning their abundance of all gifts. They boasted about their freedom from the law and traditions in matters of behavior and decorum. Paul intentionally wanted to recall the previous discussion of arrogance and boasting, and thus warn that arrogant boasting is contrary to the nature of love. It is so easy for us to fall into this trap of spiritual pride that we can't afford to neglect this warning. We employ our gifts for service and someone tells us how great we are. We believe them and become puffed up. Immediately we lose the servant spirit and our empowering.

Verses 5 and 6 are directly related to behavior, emerging from spiritual pride. Love "does not act unbecomingly." The Greek word translated "unbecomingly" occurs only twice in 1 Corinthians (here and in 7:36). An adjective derived from the same root does occur at 14:40. These references are of particular importance for our discussion. In 7:36 *ff.* Paul made mention of improper behavior toward a virgin. This is a difficult verse, but it seems likely that Paul was referring to the danger of unseemly sexual behavior between a man and his betrothed. It is possible that some of the spirituals were unduly extending the engagement period in order to boast about their spiritual ability to withstand sexual temptation. Some were not as strong as they believed and had behaved in an unacceptable manner prior to marriage.

In Chapter 14 Paul dealt with the matter of proper behavior in the worship service. Paul insisted that God was not a God of confusion. Paul demanded that there be clear guidelines for control and decency. The appeal for order in chapter 14 takes on added significance in view of 13:5. Verse 40 is not an appeal for order in worship for the sake of propriety alone, but it is an appeal to the standard of love. Love does not behave unseemly, and therefore the true spiritual will exercise his or her gift in an orderly manner precisely because he or she is controlled by love.

Unseemly behavior was nowhere more evident in Corinth than in the celebration of the Lord's Supper where there were divisions (11:-18), revelry (11:21), and a lack of concern for the poor (11:22). Earlier in chapter 11 Paul spoke of the proper behavior for the women who would pray and prophesy, and warned them against being contentious. The emphasis on freedom and disregard for tradition had led to a situation in which women were praying and prophesying with their heads uncovered. Love would never behave in these unseemly ways.

Paul probed to the very heart of Corinthian individualistic spirituality with the phrase, "does not seek its own." It is impossible to avoid the allusion to the whole controversy over idol meat as discussed in chapters 8—10. There appears to have been two closely related problems. Some Corinthians were only buying meat in the market that had been used in pagan worship while others were possibly participating in activities in a pagan temple (10:21ff.). Social events such as weddings were frequently held in the pagan temples. Paul severely warned those who were participating in the pagan worship that they might by this become sharers in demons. But the principle to which he ultimately appealed in both cases is that of responsible behavior toward others, instead of seeking one's own rights (8:13; 10:23-33). In this context Paul introduced his "right" as an apostle to receive support from his communities, only to show that he had chosen to forego this right so he might cause no hindrance to the gospel (9:12). In 10:24 and 33 the parallel with 13:5 could hardly be more apparent. "Let no one seek his own good, but that of his neighbor" (10:24). We will discover that the principle of love which seeks the good of the brethren is the controlling principle of the discussion of the use of gifts in chapter 14. Love demands that we seek gifts for ministry with others in mind (14:12) and use them accordingly.

The final two phrases of verse 5 are closely related and should be taken together. "Is not provoked" does not mean simply, "Love does not fly into a rage," but it is defined by "does not take into account a wrong suffered." Love is not embittered by injuries, real or supposed; it simply does not take them into account. Paul registered his distress at the news that the Corinthians were having lawsuits against one another before secular courts (6:6). He argued that the very fact that they have lawsuits against one another was a sign of defeat. "Why not rather be wronged? Why not rather be defrauded?" Paul pointedly asked, "Is it so, that there is not among you one wise man who will be able to decide between his brethren?" (v. 5). They were so arrogant concerning their wisdom, yet they couldn't settle simple disputes in the fellowship. Their concern for the unity of the body should have been so great that they would not "take into account a wrong suffered." The brutal facts were that the Corinthians were easily provoked with the brethren, and instead of bearing the wrong, they wanted retribution.

This comes too close to home for us to be comfortable. How often do we demand our rights when we think we have been injured by another. Do you ever find yourself keeping a mental scorecard? "I owe you one!" "I'll get you back for that one." This process of keeping count of wrongs suffered can invade the privacy of our homes. A wife is hurt by her husband's actions. She responds, "I'll forgive you this time, but don't let it happen again." She just put it in her logbook. Love is so prepared to forgive that it doesn't bother to mark the score.

Love throughout this chapter has had strong moral connotations. The final negative and its corresponding positive statement leave no question as to the importance of Christian morality. Love "does not rejoice in unrighteousness but rejoices in the truth." Most commentators point out that this phrase means that love does not rejoice over the wrongdoings committed by others or sympathize with what is evil. Paul was obviously saying that love cannot find any joy by participating in unrighteous deeds. Yet it is probable that he had even more in mind.

In chapter 5 Paul expressed his utter horror concerning the flagrant occasion of immorality in which a man was living with his stepmother. However, he was not only concerned that the deed had occurred, he was staggered by the reaction of the spirituals. Instead of mourning and taking disciplinary action, they had become arrogant (5:2,6). For this reason Paul did not simply say that love does not practice unrighteousness, but he said love "does not rejoice in unrighteousness" (see Rom. 1:32c). This is the only time that Paul used "rejoice" in a negative context. Thus Paul was not only issuing a general condemnation of their lack of regard for moral behavior, but also he was specifically calling to mind this flagrant violation of Christian morality in which the attitude of some Christians to the sin was also condemned.

Love, unlike the spirituals, rejoices in the truth. Truth here is not the truth of the gospel, but the opposite of unrighteousness. It is not surprising to find truth used with strong moral connotations (see Gal. 5:7; Eph. 4:15; 2 Thess. 2:12; John 3:21; 1 John 1:6). Paul was asserting that love rejoices in obedient, ethical behavior. The true spiritual person can never be indifferent to moral considerations. Here again we find people today who desire to give the appearance of mature spirituality, and yet use it as a cover for immoral behavior. This is an absolute contradiction in terms.

Verse 7 appears to be a more generalized statement concerning the comprehensiveness of love, and serves as a positive summary for the preceding discussion. Paul, having finished his contrast of love and the spirituals, broke into positive acclamation on the superiority of love. Not only does love avoid the exaggerated behavior patterns that were characteristic of the spirituals, but love "bears all things, believes all things, hopes all things, and endures all things." Verse 7 positively proclaims the self-giving nature of love.

The Eternal in the Now

This section is frequently overlooked, but it was Paul's most important corrective. "Love never fails" anticipates the concluding statement in verse 13. It is the positive backdrop against which the dissolution of gifts, such as prophecy, knowledge, and tongues, must be understood. Prophecies, tongues, and knowledge will pass away when the perfect comes (v. 10), but love has an eternal, timeless quality, and thus it is never invalidated in the present or future.

As I have stated, chapter 13 is Paul's "redefinition" of the spiritual person. This redefinition was developed against the mistaken understanding of spirituality already present in Corinth. The spirituals believed that they already reigned and their possession of miraculous gifts was the sign of their reign. They believed that they already possessed the fulness of the Kingdom now. Verses 8-13 touch the very heart of the matter. Paul here dealt with their overrealized eschatology in an uncompromising tone. In this section, Paul destroyed the very framework on which their spirituality had been constructed. Paul had not attempted to deny their abundance of gifts. In 13:1-3 Paul demonstrated that miraculous gifts did not authenticate their boasts to be spiritual. He asserted that love alone shows spirituality and that love was clearly lacking in the action of the spirituals.

In verses 8-13 Paul again based his argument on their "assured" abundance of miraculous gifts, but now he took a most unexpected step. He argued that their very possession of gifts for service proved the fallacy of their claim to reign spiritually. Prophecy, tongues, and so forth are earthly manifestations and thus *signs,* so to speak, of earthly existence. Remember that Paul had already established that all gifts have been given by God for the good of the brethren (12:7). He included in that discussion their prized "miraculous gifts." Their boasting had literally become their own undoing. The possession of any "spiritual gift" proved beyond any question that the spirituals did not already live in the heavenly realm, but that they belonged to the same body with all other believers. "Love," which they did not display (13:4-7), is the greatest expression of the eternal experienced by persons in the present age.

The transient nature of "spiritual manifestations" is made explicit in verse 8 with the repetition of "done away; . . . cease; . . . done away." These three particular gifts were chosen because of their prominence in Corinth, but the truth here presented holds for all gifts. All gifts are destined to pass away when the perfect comes. Obviously the gifts did not have the eternal value assigned to them by the spirituals. Consequently the possession of spiritual manifestations merely demonstrated the absurdity of the spirituals' claims to reign. Not even chapter 15 is as pointed as the argument here. It has largely gone unnoticed that this eschatological corrective was introduced with the first mention of *charismata* in 1:4-7. In verse 7 Paul echoed the boast of the spirituals to a full possession of gifts but reminded them that these gifts are for service while they await the return of the Lord.

One can hardly ignore the repetition of "in part" in verse 9 and the stark contrast between "perfect" and "partial" in verse 10. At their best, the present manifestations of prophecy and knowledge are imperfect and partial by nature and in function, a point made even more vivid by two illustrations (vv. 11-12). When "the perfect" comes, the "partial" will be rendered unnecessary. We must ask what Paul meant by "the perfect." The word "child" in verse 11 has caused some commentators to suggest that "perfect" means Christian maturity, but this is to misunderstand the illustrative purpose of verse 11 and to ignore the context. Knowing in part, for example, will be done away with when we see face to face (v. 12). Paul did not have in mind the Christian coming to perfection but spoke of the *perfect* (the consummation of the age) which will come to replace the *partial*. Other scholars have suggested that "perfect" refers to the end of the age of the apostles or the writing of the Scripture. The term *perfect* is not used elsewhere in these ways and such an interpretation misses the point of this entire section. Paul was quite willing to accept their boast to an abundance of gifts. He wanted to correct the assertion that they were "signs" that they reigned. The "perfect" is the end of the age. When Christ returns, gifts will have no value because then we will see face to face and know as we are known.

The gifts do have a value, but they must be evaluated in terms of their role in the present stage of redemptive history. They are manifestations of the *now*, and thus are limited to and by the present age. When the perfect comes, there will be full participation in the Kingdom, but ironically (for the spirituals) this will mean the demise of the gifts as they are now experienced.

The illustration of childhood/maturity should be taken at face value. Speaking, thinking, and reasoning refer only to normal functions and are not to be understood as references to tongues, prophecy, and knowledge. The term "child" here has no negative connotations. Childish thinking and behavior are not evil; they are simply inadequate or partial in comparison with mature functions. The adult sets aside immature childish ways of thinking and responding, not out of disdain for them but because they have been surpassed by maturity. The spiritual manifestations of this age, no matter how magnificent they may seem now, will be seen as childish in comparison with the fullness to be possessed when the Kingdom is fully realized. Paul did not suggest that they put away these gifts now, for that would be contrary to what he had taught in chapter 12. He did, however, insist that they view them in the *proper perspective*. They are manifestations of God's grace that enables the believer to minister for the good of the body. This truth will determine which gifts should be eagerly sought and that is the topic of chapter 14.

A second illustration presents a more pointed contrast between the nature of the manifestations of the "now" and the fullness of the "then." This illustration is heightened by the repetition of "then" and "now." The spirituals apparently claimed direct revelational knowledge which gave them insights into the great "mysteries" of the faith and also into daily affairs. We noticed this in regard to food offered to idols. Paul agreed that Christians do have a deeper understanding of spiritual things and a special insight into God's will (ch. 2) through the revelation of the Holy Spirit. Yet the spirituals were not simply claiming to have knowledge, but to possess "all knowledge" (1:5 and cf. 13:2). This was their proof that they already reigned. Paul countered by demonstrating that present knowledge was like the dim image in a mirror, whereas the knowing when the Kingdom is *fully experienced* would be like seeing face to face. Paul had already warned them that despite their boasts, no one yet knows as he ought to know (8:2).

The metaphor of seeing in a mirror was common in Paul's time. Paul used this readily available metaphor for his own purposes. Mirrors of the day were not as refined as ours today. The image was often dim or distorted. The phrase "we see in a mirror dimly" is explained by "*now* I know in part." "*Then* face to face" is paralleled by "*then* I shall know *fully* just as I also have been fully known" (author's italics). Although the whole section is corrective, knowing *dimly* is not a fault. Present knowledge by its very nature is partial. Consequently it will be obscure or unclear when contrasted with knowledge when the perfect comes. Again remember that Paul was merely demonstrating the "partial" and "earthly" nature of all present manifestations.

We must recognize that the arguments which attempt to make perfect mean the end of the age of the apostles or the end of the revelation of the Scriptures miss the real thrust of this section. Many commentators have argued in this manner so that they might suggest that tongues ceased with the end of the apostolic age. Logically, we would further be forced to say that knowledge and prophecy ceased. I'm not sure we would be as anxious to see an end to these gifts, particularly when we discover Paul's preference for prophecy in chapter 14. But all such arguments actually miss the real thrust of this entire chapter. The possession of any of these gifts demonstrated the foolishness of their boasts to an exalted spiritual status. Gifts do not possess any *sign* value, they possess only *service* value.

Paul concluded this chapter with an exclamation on the superiority of love. "But now," in contrast to the spiritual manifestations, there remain eternally, faith, hope, and love. "Remain" reiterates the idea of "Love never fails" (v. 8) and thus contrasts with the repeated "done away." Faith, hope, and love alone of those things active in the present have eternal significance. Nevertheless, Paul's emphasis is on love, and thus it is proclaimed to be the greatest of the three. But why are faith and hope introduced at all? Faith, hope, and love are frequently found linked in the Pauline letters and the triad probably reflects a recognized formula created by the early church or by Paul himself. Paul simply utilized the familiar formula to heighten his teaching but underlined love because of the particular emphasis of this passage.

The claim to spirituality based on miraculous gifts was demonstrated to be invalid because gifts are limited to earthly existence, and the greatest eternal reality available in the now had been found to be conspicuously lacking in the behavior of the spirituals. By emphasizing the eschatological reality of love, Paul gave a new dimension to the affairs of everyday life. While chapter 13 denies gifts a sign value, it does not render the gifts worthless. On the contrary, now they can be seen in the *proper perspective*. Gifts of grace are manifestations of the *now*, and thus their real meaning is discovered only when they are used by the "spiritual person," as defined in chapter 13 to express the eschatological reality of love in the now. More simply put, spiritual gifts have meaning only when they are used for the edification of the body. Therefore chapters 12 and 13 prepare the way for the practical discussion of the function of the gifts of grace in the Corinthian community (ch. 14).

Notes

1. *Glossolalia* is a word derived from two Greek words, *glōssa* and *laleō,* and means literally "to speak tongues." It is used commonly to refer to speaking in tongues.

2. This is made more plausible by the likelihood that the saying recorded in Luke 20:34-36 was being used by some in Corinth to defend the ascetic life-style.

5
The Spiritual Person Seeking Spiritual Gifts

Pursue Love and Desire Gifts

I believe I'm beginning to understand what you're getting at, Paul. Gifts do not prove anything about the possessor. They don't show that I'm baptized in the Spirit or have any special merit. They simply prove that God is gracious in gifting His church for any and every task it faces. I can see now that I have actually been limiting the work of the Spirit in terms of the variety of gifts that I have been willing to recognize. You tell me that gifts are given to edify the body and love will concretely express itself in edifying behavior. Can you give me some suggestions now on which gifts I should seek? A second concern you might address: with all the gifted members in the congregation, how do we control the exercise of the gifts? To tell you the truth it gets a little out of hand around here occasionally.

Obviously, you recognize that the preceding is a ficticious response to Paul. This seems to me to be the response that Paul would have desired from the Corinthians. You will notice that these very topics were the concerns which Paul focused on in chapter 14.

Once you have grasped the flow of Paul's thought, you will clearly understand that "Pursue love, yet desire earnestly spiritual gifts, but especially that you may prophesy" (14:1) is the natural linking that brings this whole subject to a practical conclusion. Paul first presented a radically new interpretation of the manifestations of the Spirit in chapter 12 and then he redefined the spiritual man in terms of one whose life-style is determined by *agape* (ch. 13). These two insights

92

are forcefully brought together in 14:1 with the close juxtaposition of "pursue love" and "desire earnestly spiritual gifts" (*pneumatika*). Paul now applied the teaching of chapters 12 and 13 in a practical fashion by demonstrating how the spiritual person would respond to the needs of the brethren in seeking and utilizing the gifts. The discussion of chapter 14 is intensely practical.

When you first read 1 Corinthians 14 the word that will stand out in your mind is *edification.* Paul used this term to bring the spirituals back to earth. The gifts were given for the common good, and it is in the life of the body that the gifts can be used most effectively to minister to others. While it is true that Paul wanted to call the spirituals back to the historical reality of the *now;* he did, nevertheless, give a way that gifts can be used in such a way as to have *eternal* significance. Spiritual persons can utilize their "earthly gifts" (13:8-13) in the *now* to express the eternal reality of love (cf. 1:8). Love expressed through the gifts is experienced in terms of edification (cf. 8:1), and accordingly edification is at the heart of chapter 14. When *agape* is the controlling force of the individual, the zeal to edify (14:12) will always be determinative of one's desire and employment of gifts. To put it another way: gifts of grace provide the vehicle through which the spiritual person can communicate love to others.

One might ask at this point, "Why did Paul use *pneumatika* (spiritual gifts) again in 14:1 if it had implications he wanted to correct?" This is at first sight a difficult question, and it is a question which is often neglected by those who would distinguish between *pneumatika* and *charismata.* The answer lies in the correct understanding of desire earnestly (*zēloō*) spiritual gifts (*pneumatika*). Once again Paul used the language and thought of the spirituals to highlight his own teaching (see 12:31; 14:12). He intentionally returned to their terminology and discussed two of the valued *pneumatika* for several reasons:

(1) Paul was eager to make his corrective on common ground with the spirituals. The strength of this approach is obvious—the conclusions become unavoidably relevant for Corinth; (2) Paul's corrective was thus designed to have immediate practical results for the Corin-

thian worship service, which was apparently in need of direction; (3) He demonstrated again that he was not simply disparaging the *pneumatika* (miraculous gifts), an objection which Paul anticipated (see 14:18 *ff.*); (4) Prophecy and glossolalia were contrasted in this chapter for two distinct reasons. First, they were both popular gifts in Corinth, and thus they were being abused by the spirituals. Paul wanted to demonstrate how the spiritual person concerned about expressing love could employ these two gifts for the common good (14:26 *ff.*). Second, out of all the *pneumatika* these two gifts, because they share both similarities and differences, provided the best contrast by which Paul could make clear his point concerning "the greater gifts" (12:31).

In one sense these two gifts and their proper use are discussed, but in a greater sense these two gifts are used in a representative fashion, and the conclusions reached in relation to these two gifts can be applied to all gifts. It is not insignificant that anytime I speak on spiritual gifts the number-one question relates to tongues. It seems to hold the same fascination for believers today that it held for the Corinthians. It has that miraculous and mysterious quality which creates such interest that many folks simply miss the real point of chapter 14. The fact that our needs and concerns are similar to the Corinthians perhaps gives us the final clue as to why Paul felt compelled to deal with this matter in such detail in chapter 14.

Here a question of some importance arises. If the gifts are distributed by the Spirit as He wills, how can Paul suggest that one should seek a certain gift (12:31; 14:1, 12,39)? It should be remembered that the purpose of 12:11 was to forestall arrogance concerning the possession of any gifts and not to suggest that one should not seek certain gifts. The fact that gifts for ministry are given does not mean that they cannot be sought. It is similar in principle to the whole issue of prayer. In Matthew 6:8 Jesus told His disciples that the Father knew their needs before they asked. Yet in the same context He gave specific instructions for asking concerning our needs. In this context we must keep in mind Paul's personalized concept of the Spirit. The sovereignty of the Giver does not negate human responsibility in the asking.

Paul's emphasis on zealously desiring the greater gifts (12:31) was called for by the Corinthian difficulties. Nevertheless it was based on the conviction that God desires to grant gifts for the edification of the body.

The Role of Prophecy and Tongues

The phrase "especially that you may prophesy" in 14:1 directs the reader's thought back to 12:31 and the emphasis on greater gifts. The answer as to which gifts are greater was foreshadowed in 12:21-24, and given eschatological basis in chapter 13, but is made explicit here. The greater gifts, simply stated, are those which are best suited for edifying the community. "Greater" is a general category and does not anticipate a detailed ranking which would describe one gift as slightly greater than another. Greater in terms of edifying capacity was set over against the spirituals' assessment of greater in terms of sign value. With the phrase, "especially that you may prophesy," Paul established the priority of prophecy and in a representative sense the priority of all edifying gifts (see 14:12).

The intelligibility of prophecy and the unintelligibility of tongues is the controlling thought of the first 25 verses. The connective word *for* in verse 2 suggests that the content of verse 2 concerning tongues should be understood in the light of the overarching concern of Paul expressed by the phrase "especially that you may prophesy." The statement that the one speaking in a tongue speaks to God is not to be understood, in the first instance, as a positive affirmation concerning tongue speech, but as a contrast to the prophet who speaks to men for edification.[1] It must be remembered that Paul was establishing the priority of prophecy in terms of intelligibility.

The emphasis in this verse falls on "no one understands" which does not mean that the tongues were inaudible, but they were unintelligible. Likewise the phrase, "in his spirit he speaks mysteries" must be interpreted in light of the entire context. Some commentators argue that "mysteries" here, as elsewhere in Paul, means the divine mysteries of God's plan of salvation. But as most commentators note, the context suggests a negative connotation. "In his spirit he speaks mysteries" explains the phrase "no one understands." The tongue speaker, therefore, was contrasted with the prophet who "speaks to men for edification" (14:3). Glossolalia, uninterpreted, is simply a mystery to the hearer. It should be noted that G. G. Findlay argued that the "normal" meaning of mysteries is maintained and that 14:2 is negative. The mysteries of God are worth hearing and therefore should be rationally spoken. Glossolalia alone stops short, merely tantalizing the church.[2] Since glossolalia can be edifying if interpreted, this suggestion cannot be excluded.

In contrast to the one who speaks in tongues, the prophet speaks to people to edify, exhort, and comfort. Since edification is the primary concern of this chapter, it is possible that exhortation and comfort are intended to explain edification. It is likewise possible that the three terms are used simply to strengthen the contrast between prophecy and glossolalia. In Romans 12:8 "exhortation" is listed as a charismatic ability separate from prophecy. Remember also that Paul encouraged the Thessalonians to undertake these tasks in regard to one another (1 Thess. 5:11; 5:14). In the Thessalonian letter they were not treated as gifts. The major point is clear: prophecy, because it is intelligible is "greater" in terms of its ability to edify the church.

Having described prophecy and glossolalia, Paul (v. 4) compared the edifying value of each of these gifts. The contrast between "edifies himself" and "edifies the church" is consistent with the preceding descriptions and leads to the conclusion in verse 5. In the light of verses 4, 17, and 28b, it can hardly be denied that Paul acknowledged that tongues could have a positive personal value. It must be noted that although "edifies himself" in verse 4 was not primarily intended to establish a beneficial aspect of glossolalia, it may in fact point out what Paul believed to be a positive function of this gift. It has value for private devotions. Nevertheless, in the light of the Corinthian problems and the present context we must not ignore earlier injunctions such as "let no one seek his own good, but that of his neighbor" (10:24 and see 33) and "does not seek its own" (13:5). Edifying oneself is admittedly pale in contrast to the possibility of edifying the church. Consequently the emphasis in this verse is on especially seeking prophecy. This is still the focal point for understanding the flow of Paul's argument. His main emphasis was on the value of these two gifts in the center of the gathered community, and not their value for personal devotions.

Verse 5 was not a concession to those in Corinth who would assert the importance of tongues, nor was it straightforward praise of tongues. The emphasis in this verse is on "even more" (*mallon,* same Greek word as 14:1), and thus the contrast of the preceding verse is still being advanced. Therefore, "I wish that you all spoke in tongues" should not be interpreted literally as if Paul desired a universal practice of tongues or prophecy. We've already established that all do not speak with tongues or prophecy (12:29-30). The reference in 14:23-24 is to a hypothetical case, *used for emphasis,* and 14:31a in context refers to all those who have the gift of prophecy. A literal interpretation would not only contradict 12:29-30 but it would go against the thrust of chapter 12 where Paul insisted on the divine necessity of variety.

First Corinthians 14:5 was not intended to tell us anything about the universality of either of these gifts. At this juncture, the representative function of these two gifts is not far below the surface. Consequently Paul was not suggesting that all should seek the gift of prophecy exclusively (see 12:17), but he was dramatically contrasting the importance of seeking gifts which are better suited to edification (like prophecy) in contrast to those which are more dramatic but less edifying (like tongues).

Paul continued the comparison of the one prophesying and the one speaking in tongues and added a warning concerning tongues which is important for the proper understanding of several sections of this chapter. Because the one prophesying edifies the congregation (14:3), he is greater than the one who speaks in tongues, "unless" the tongues speaker himself interprets so that the congregation might be edified. Both the natural reading of the Greek and the context lead to the conclusion that Paul expected the tongues speaker who was concerned for edification to interpret his own speech. If one possessed the gift of tongues and desired to use it for the good of the body by interpreting it, and not simply as a banner of spirituality, then he/she would be equal to the prophet. It is not that the gift of tongues plus interpretation is equal to prophecy, but that the tongues speaker who interprets functions in an edifying fashion as does the prophet. Verse 13 supports this interpretation. Paul expected the tongues speakers to pray for the gift of interpretation. I am aware that this is opposite of what is taught and practiced in most charismatic groups. If you will follow the explanation of the entire passage I think you will see that this is the logical interpretation of verses 13 *ff.*

Intelligibility Illustrated

Verses 6-8 contain rhetorical questions, the answers to which are readily apparent. Using himself as an example, Paul first asked how he could benefit them if he came speaking a tongue. The obvious point is that Paul could be of benefit to them only if he spoke intelligibly—by means of a revelation, knowledge, prophecy, or teaching. The context makes it clear that by "revelation" Paul did not mean tongues plus interpretation. It is difficult and unnecessary at this point to distinguish closely between the four types of *intelligible* speech. The main point is clear: although Paul could come to them and win acceptance with a demonstration of his spectacular abilities, he preferred to speak intelligibly in order to edify.

The argument here and in verses 18-19 is not unrelated to Paul's insistence that the spiritual person would gladly forfeit his own rights for the opportunity to help others. Since tongues alone are unintelligible and thus do not edify, the spiritual person (redefined in chapter 13) would gladly forfeit the right to a public display of tongues.

Paul substantiated his emphasis on intelligibility by two practical illustrations which grow in intensity. What is the value of even a lifeless instrument, if it does not give distinct notes? There is nothing to suggest that Paul was alluding to 13:1, although it is possible that the Corinthians themselves may have made the connection. If a musical instrument is played but with no distinction of notes, the exercise is futile and possibly even offensive to one who appreciates music. The illustration that always comes to my mind is the child who has just taken up playing the violin unknown to her father. The dad is calmly watching the Sunday afternoon game when the screeching and scratching commences. Startled, he leaps from his chair to see who is dying only to greet the smiling face of his daughter who proudly proclaims she's making music. An instrument played with no distinction of notes is not harmful, but it can be annoying. With the trumpet, however, the indistinct sound is even more problematic. No one will prepare for battle, and thus the results will be confusion and inactivity. An indistinct sound in this case can be dangerous.

The strength of the words "so also you" (v. 9) must not be minimized. Paul was applying the preceding argument to the Corinthian situation. The reference to human language placed the argument at the highest level. Unless one used his human tongue for intelligible communication, it was as futile as speaking into the air (see 9:26). If it was important for a lifeless instrument to produce intelligible sounds, how much more important is it for the Corinthians to produce intelligible sounds with their physical tongues. Therefore, even though Paul did not refer to glossolalia in this verse, it is not difficult to see that the abuse of that gift was in mind.

Verse 9 flows naturally into verses 10 and 11 where human language is still in view. Paul conceded that there was no human language which did not have a meaning. Perhaps Paul was meeting an anticipated reply of the spirituals: "But our 'tongues' cannot be likened to an indistinct note of an instrument; they are the languages of the angels (13:1)." Whatever Paul's opinion on the content of tongue speech, he here insisted that even valid languages have no meaning if they are not understood.[3] The speaker and the hearer will be like barbarians to one another. The term *barbarian* was probably intended to be somewhat derogatory. The unintelligible tongues, which were a great source of pride for the spirituals, would not lead others to praise them as spiritual persons. On the contrary, persons who could not understand the tongues would regard the speakers as barbarians (see 14:23). Paul removed both the sign value of tongues and demonstrated their lack of ability to edify the hearer.

Seek to Abound for Edification

The repetition of the emphatic "So also you" in verse 12 (see v. 9) made the application pointed. Paul pressed home his point by alluding to their zealous nature and attaching his corrective to their terminology. This is the clearest statement of Paul's main corrective in this chapter.

Paul's first concern was not simply to exalt prophecy, but to direct their zeal for and use of all gifts toward the goal of edification. Zealousness for gifts in Corinth could be a good thing as long as gifts were properly understood as God's gracious manifestations given for the upbuilding of the body. This should be the controlling factor in a person's "seeking" a particular gift. One must ask, "Do I desire this gift for selfish reasons, or for reasons of edification?" This same question is relevant today.

You will notice in verse 12 the words *spiritual gifts.* You may be wondering, Did Paul use their word *pneumatika* or his corrective term *charismata?* Those who read the Greek will find that Paul simply used a plural form of *pneuma* (Spirit). It is best to understand this as being equivalent to *pneumatika.* It is likely that Paul was here again using the actual words of the Corinthians, as has frequently been the case in this letter. What then did the use of the plural form of *pneuma* mean in this passage? Some have suggested that the Corinthians may have believed that the gifts were mediated by the angels, whose language they spoke. If so, the emphasis on *one Spirit* in chapter 12 is important. I think it is more likely that the Corinthians were using popular terminology but with no real distinction between these words.

We can argue with greater assurance that Paul's emphasis was on the corrective: "seek to abound for the edification of the church." Paul had already demonstrated that the *charismata* were given by God for the common good. Here he moved a step further: true spiritual persons will seek to abound in gifts so that they might edify the church. Notice the continued emphasis on abundance. The spirituals wanted to abound for the wrong reasons. This had affected the kind of gifts they had been zealous to possess. If their desire to abound could be

Emphasis on Abundance

redirected toward edification, then it follows that it would affect their "selection" of gifts.

I have often heard people ask jokingly, "Would you rather cool down a charismatic, or warm up a corpse?" The obvious suggestion is that charismatics have much zeal and many traditional churches are dead. Unfortunately, there often is more truth to that than we like to confess. I think we all have, from time to time, looked on the zeal of charismatic friends with a bit of envy, wondering why they seem to be so excited about their faith. Paul's desire was not to put out the zeal, but to redirect it toward edifying behavior rather than emotional showmanship. Certainly God's desire would be for us to discover the zeal given by His Spirit but to allow it to move us to service for our fellow human beings.

The Use of Tongues in the Assembly

Someone has said, "Anytime you find a 'therefore' in Scripture, you need to determine what it is there for." The *therefore* in verse 13 ties this next section to the principle stated in verse 12. The implicit question is: "How can the person with the gift of tongues use the gift for the edification of the body? Paul suggested in verse 5 that the tongues speaker could edify like the prophet if he would interpret.

Here Paul was more explicit: "Therefore—that is to say if the tongues speaker is zealous to edify—let one who speaks in a tongue pray that he may interpret." The prayer was in normal language, and its content was the petition that the person might receive the gift of interpretation so that he might edify the church (vv. 16-17). When we follow the logical content of this chapter the most obvious interpretation of verse 13 is the one suggested above. The objection to this interpretation is the common assumption that not all tongues speakers were expected to interpret. What is the basis for this common assumption that the one who spoke in tongues usually did (or does) not possess the gift of interpretation. Does this text imply that?[4]

Leaving aside 14:27-28 for the moment, the natural meaning of verses 5 and 13 is that tongues speakers should interpret. Nonetheless, it is probably accurate to say that few tongues speakers in Corinth interpreted their tongues or even desired to do so. It was the language of angels, and to render it intelligible would lessen its sign value. By commanding (imperative verb) the tongues speaker to pray that he might interpret, Paul demonstrated that this gift like others was a manifestation of this age and as such should be used for the edification of the church. Those who already possessed the gift of tongues and desired to utilize it authentically should pray for the ability to interpret. Conversely, those tongue speakers who continued to exercise their gifts with no view to edification would demonstrate thereby that they are not truly spiritual persons.

According to this interpretation of verse 13, verses 14-17 are best understood as practical instructions for the use of tongues plus interpretation in the assembly. This line of interpretation is congenial to the context as a whole and provides for a meaningful transition to verse 15. One immediately notes the elementary nature of the instructions. This may indicate that interpretation of tongues was not practiced at Corinth, and that Paul had not given the Corinthians any previous instructions for the use of tongues in the assembly.

In verse 14 Paul gave a straightforward appraisal of what takes place when one prays in a tongue. The contrast in verses 13-16 is between *spirit* and *mind.* This contrast is repeated in verse 19 as "in a tongue" and "with my mind." In the light of the personalized references to spirit (my spirit) and its subordination to mind, it is unlikely that it means "Holy Spirit." The contrast throughout this section is between two states of consciousness, and therefore I take "spirit" to mean the human spirit which can be transported into ecstasy.

The contrast therefore is between speaking in a rational state of consciousness and in an altered state of consciousness, or ecstasy. The phrases were used descriptively, and no qualitative judgment was intended. Paul did not mean to imply that speaking in tongues was the work of the Spirit, whereas prophecy or teaching was a rational exercise devoid of the Spirit. Still more, Paul was not suggesting that religious ecstasy was to be avoided. Paul did subordinate the ecstatic experience to the rational when the edification of the body was at stake. Paul underlined this point in 2 Corinthians 5:13: "For if we are beside ourselves, it is for God; if we are of sound mind, it is for you."

Religious ecstasy is experienced in different ways by different people. Some are moved by music, some through prayer, and so forth. It is a genuine but highly personalized experience. It is something God grants to us for our own edification. The results of ecstasy are such that they are not easily shared. It is much like the experience you have when you go on vacation and you encounter that breathtaking view. You can't wait to share this experience with your friends when you return. With great excitement you tell of your great find. By the look on their faces, you see they're not moved by your experience. You respond to their lack of facial response: "I guess you had to be there." That is precisely the point of religious ecstasy—it is a personal gift of God. Its contents are not easily shared. It has a place, but it is not intended to be the focal point of the worship service.

You will recall that in 2 Corinthians 10—13 Paul had been challenged by teachers who were boasting in their visions. Apparently they were basing their teaching on messages received during a vision. Paul finally shared that he too had experienced a vision, and while he heard words, they were inexpressible (2 Cor. 12:1-4). He had been unable to communicate the content of his vision. It was given him for his own edification. The danger of ecstasy occurs when we try to live on the ecstatic, attempt to recreate the atmosphere for ecstasy, or base our teaching upon ecstasy.

There are some Sunday mornings when our congregational singing is such that it sends chills up my spine. The whole service just flows from there. I am often tempted to say to our minister of music: "Let's do the service just like that next week." But it won't be the same! You can't demand or create ecstasy. We've all been guilty of attempting to do so. We think if we can just get back to that retreat center or our home church, we'll restore that feeling. If we pray long enough or sing loud enough, ecstasy will surely come. We're like Elijah of old who thought God could only speak in the fire, wind, or earthquake (1 Kings 19:12). We're surprised that He is also heard in the still small voice of solitude. Ecstatic experience is the sovereign act of God, given for our personal edification.

In the ecstatic experience of tongues, the mind of the individual who prays in tongues remains unfruitful, that is, the sounds which he utters have no rational content for him. The Christian who has this gift and wants to use it for the common good will first pray or sing in his tongue and then interpret his prayer by praying or singing with the mind so that he might edify all by making his message intelligible. If one blesses in the spirit *only*, how can the "ungifted" say the "Amen"? "The one who fills the place of the ungifted" is used figuratively to refer to a Christian who is unskilled in tongues and interpretation. We know this refers to a believer because Paul was concerned that this individual be able to understand and be edified by the teaching. The hearers signified their agreement with the prayer by saying "Amen." They could make this response only if they were fully aware of its content. "You are giving thanks well enough" can be taken at face value. The tongues speaker may give thanks quite well in his uninterpreted tongue, but he does not edify. But edification is the primary concern for gathered worship.

These instructions were followed by a boast which was intended as a sharp corrective to those who exalt the worth of tongues in the gathered assembly—even tongues plus interpretation. Paul had just given directions for the use of tongues plus interpretation in the assembly, now by using himself as an example he showed a strong preference for the non-ecstatic, intelligible speech in gathered worship. Paul may have anticipated the objection that he was minimizing ecstatic gifts, particularly tongues, because he lacked them. Therefore, he testified that he could thank God that he possessed tongues in greater abundance than they did. The boast in this instance closely parallels the argumentation of 2 Corinthians 10—13. In that passage the issue was visionary experiences. Paul had not wanted to share his own visionary experience as he considered it a very personal moment of ecstasy which could not be communicated. In both places the argument was developed in such a manner that it causes us to suspect that the Corinthians were not aware that Paul had experienced tongues or visions. Paul, who possessed their highly-valued spiritual manifestations, voluntarily refrained from publicly displaying them so that he might seek the advantage of the many (see 1 Cor. 9; 10:33 to 11:1). Paul had sacrificed what the spirituals might have considered to be his rights. Paul did so for their good. The effect of this verse depended on the fact that they did not know of Paul's practice of tongues. He had ministered there for eighteen months and had not shared concerning this gift of tongues because he viewed it as a personal experience of ecstasy. Paul's preference in the assembly of believers was for intelligible speech which could edify the entire assembly.

The Danger of Tongues and the Unbeliever

Most pastors and teachers have found verses 20-25 to be very difficult to follow. The passage is obviously central to Paul's entire argument, yet it is fraught with difficulties. Why did Paul use this quotation of Isaiah, and what is its relationship to the present context? Why did Paul call prophecy a sign for believers and then proceed to talk about its effect on nonbelievers? There are other numerous small matters of debate such as the identity of the "ungifted" (*idiōtes*) and the relationship between the unbelievers in verses 22 and 24. Many of these problems are the direct result of trying to read more into this passage than it was actually intended to convey. We must determine the intent of the passage in light of the Corinthian situation.

There can be little doubt that verses 20-25 continue the argument against the immature overevaluation of tongues and their arrogant display in the assembly. In verse 20, Paul virtually reversed the spirituals' view of themselves. They believed themselves to be mature and to abound in wisdom and knowledge, but Paul exhorted them: "Do not be children in your thinking, . . . but in your thinking be mature." In one stroke Paul attacked their understanding of themselves as "spirituals," and "mature" (*teleloi*) and countered their claims to excel in wisdom and knowledge. They had demonstrated childish judgment by their zealousness to possess the ecstatic gifts rather than more edifying gifts. They did so because they believed them to be signs that they were "spiritual persons." This was not an evil decision, just a childish one. Their judgment concerning the nature and relative value of manifestations of the Spirit had proved that they were still children.

My family has developed a tradition which has proved to be a fun but sometimes frustrating outing. Each year, a few weeks before Christmas, I give our children some money to buy gifts for other family members. I am always amused that they tend to choose the shiniest item replete with lights, bells, and whistles. This choice is sometimes accompanied by the innocent: "Won't Mom be surprised!" I have, at times, attempted to intervene and suggest a more appropriate and practical gift for Mom. This has usually been met with the objection: "Oh, Dad, that's boring!" I can only smile knowingly because I used to do the same thing every Christmas. The affection for the showy and shiny is just a part of childish enthusiasm. Paul was confronting a similar childlike enthusiasm for the spectacular and showy. The edifying gifts could look boring in comparison.

The comment concerning moral innocence of the child was itself pointed and calculated to recall the import of chapter 13. Whereas the spirituals had divorced ethical behavior and spiritual manifestations, Paul brought the two together into the closest possible connection. The spiritual person would be characterized by love and he would recognize the manifestations of the Spirit as what they were, *charismata,* given for the common good. This should, in turn, lead to a desire for edifying gifts.

Paul now cited Isaiah 28:11-12 in the form slightly different from the Old Testament text. This verse was used by Paul as a direct confrontation of the use of tongues as a sign of spirituality. The Isaiah passage probably attracted Paul's attention because of its reference to men of other tongues and because it could easily be used to give a negative appraisal of the sign value of tongues.

I suspect that Paul's use of this text to prove that tongues were not a sign for believers was surprising to the Corinthians and was therefore made more effective. So it is unnecessary to harmonize the meaning of Isaiah 28:11 *ff.* in its original context and its use here. Paul simply used this Old Testament passage to fortify his bold assertion that tongues were *not* a sign for believers. Paul had been insistent throughout the entire letter that miraculous gifts did not have sign value. To their surprise, Paul now allowed that tongues, were for a sign, but for *unbelievers* not for believers. We need not press Paul's argument by insisting for more than he actually stated. The single point of this statement is that tongues are *not a sign for believers!*

Paul balanced this negative statement on tongues as a sign gift by adding that prophecy *is a sign for believers*. The point made is a simple one in agreement with the thrust of the entire chapter. Prophecy is a sign for believers because of its value for the life of the church. The illustration in verses 23-25 confirms this interpretation.

It is unnecessary and confusing to carry forward the mention of sign value when interpreting verses 23-24. The sign terminology was used simply to refute the spirituals' appeal to gifts as a sign and to confirm the argument that the true spiritual will prefer edifying gifts.

Paul now offered a practical illustration to demonstrate the superior value of prophecy in the assembly. He first suggested a hypothetical situation in which the church comes together and speaking in tongues occurs. The reference to "all" in both verse 23 and verse 24 was used to give vivid impact to the illustration. It was not intended to convey the idea that all are speaking at the same time. All prophesying at the same time would be as confusing as all speaking in tongues. Nor did it mean that Paul envisaged the possibility that everyone in the church might possess either prophecy or tongues. Paul had already spoken to this issue.

The reader was now shown the negative response of both the "un-gifted" and the "unbeliever" to tongues spoken in the assembly. The order of these two terms in verses 23-24 is important. In verse 23 "ungifted" occurs first. The reader is reminded of the reaction to tongues by the ungifted as mentioned in verse 16. *Ungifted* simply means one who is unskilled in the specific matter being discussed. If the Christian who lacks this gift responds negatively, what will be the response of the unbelievers? The term *mad* (*mainomai*) was chosen to provide the most striking contrast possible between the results of prophecy and tongues. It is possible that there may have been an implied warning that they must be careful lest their ecstasy be mistaken for pagan enthusiasm. The meaning here is not unlike the implied point of verse 11. The true impact of the public demonstration of dramatic gifts was quite the opposite of what the spirituals had envisioned. Perhaps a part of Paul's reluctance for a public display of tongues, even with interpretation, in the assembly was the fear that the outsider would be so adversely affected by the tongue speech that he would react against Christianity or simply regard it as another enthusiastic cult.

Given the same situation, the response to prophecy will be positive. The order is reversed and prophecy's effect on the unbeliever is considered first. If the effects on the unbeliever are as beneficial as this, they will also be beneficial in relation to the Christian without the gift of prophecy. The three prositive phrases "he is convicted by all," "he is called to account by all," and "the secrets of his heart are disclosed" are placed over against the single phrase "will they not say that you are mad?" Remember Paul had already used a threefold comparison in 14:2-3. The end result of prophecy was that the unbeliever was converted.

Paul was not specifically describing the prophetic task, but illustrating prophecy's greater value. It is doubtful that Paul was suggesting a type of thought-reading whereby the prophet publicly called out the specific sins of an unbeliever. Paul simply pointed out that because prophecy was intelligible, it would bring conviction of sin and the distinct awareness of the presence of God. The contrast is between "will they not say you are mad" and "declaring that God is certainly among you." Which is to be preferred?

There is one question which emerges quite clearly from 14:1-25 and which requires some attention before we move to the practical instructions of 14:26 *ff*. How can tongues be treated as a gift of grace? The *charismata* are given for the common good, but tongues alone cannot edify the body. Remember that in 12:10 Paul listed tongues and interpretation as separate gifts. While Paul saw tongues and interpretation as separate gifts, he anticipated that the true spiritual, who possessed tongues and wanted to edify the church, could pray for and receive the companion gift of interpretation. Thus, even though one not gifted in tongues might possess the gift of interpretation, every tongues speaker could and should possess it. This alleviates our dilemma to some extent, but it does not solve it. Tongues alone was listed as a gift, but alone it cannot serve the common good.

We should also note that Paul treated glossolalia with reserve in 1 Corinthians 14 and did not specifically mention it in any other letter. It appears that Paul viewed tongues, visionary experiences, and other such ecstatic experiences as having some value for the individual (1 Cor. 14:2,4,17,28*b;* 2 Cor. 5:13 and 12:1 *ff.*), but little value for the assembled church. Nevertheless, Paul provisionally and with some difficulty made a place for and attempted to control tongues in the worship service in Corinth, because of its prevalence there. We'll discover these controls in the next section. Paul would not ban tongues outright in the service because that would have only served to alienate the spirituals. He wanted to redirect their zeal not crush their enthusiasm. Second, Paul was sensitive to the working of the Spirit and was cautious lest he be guilty of hindering the Spirit's work.

Directions for Assembled Worship

"What is the outcome then brethren" introduces a new but related matter. Paul applied the insights of his previous teaching in order to give much needed practical guidelines to the Corinthian worship service. This section clearly had in mind the specific difficulties of Corinth, and therefore one must be cautious about making overgeneralized conclusions from this passage about worship and its control in the early church. The gathered worship service was of little consequence to the spirituals, except as a ready forum where they could demonstrate their valued gifts. It was by making the gifts *serviceable* and *answerable* to this assembly of believers that Paul corrected the spirituals' abuse of spiritual manifestations.

We should not fail to notice that we have now come full circle. We are ready to pick up the thought of 12:7. The emphasis in both passages is on each believer and the good of the whole. Every individual could contribute to the corporate worship if his or her aim was to edify. This entire section was designed to silence any arrogant display which did not have as its aim the good of the body. The list of gifts in verse 26 is not comprehensive, nor is the order significant. The things mentioned are those which might be expected in gathered worship and focus around teaching. It is unnecessary for our present purpose to describe the various activities. The only new item is "psalm" which may refer to the ability to compose a song, or simply the ability to praise the Lord in song. In either case the songs were such that all can be edified (see Col. 3:16). The range of abilities which were discussed here under charismatic functioning is impressively broad. Notice however that the discussion again centers on tongues and prophecy.

The discussion of the practical use of tongues and prophecy was framed by reference to edification (v.26) and to peace (v.33*a*). Did Paul therefore impose rationalistic practical controls on the spiritual gifts, or are the participants themselves expected to exercise restraint? As will become apparent, Paul spoke of both external and internal control. The twin convictions that God is not a God of confusion and that the true spiritual will seek to edify the church (14:12) are intertwined throughout this section.

Paul limited the tongues speakers to two or three "in turn" and that accompanied by interpretation. Our understanding of this passage is somewhat limited by our inability to fully reconstruct the practice of tongues plus interpretation. This is the only passage which specifically touches upon the subject, and thus we must draw from our understanding of the Corinthian situation and from the larger instruction of this chapter. We know that tongues was a valued gift in Corinth for its sign value because of its mysterious and spectacular nature. It is unlikely that the spirituals had sought to control the use of tongues in any way since they had given no thought to edification. Tongues must now be looked at with the view to the common good in mind.

The phrase translated in the NASB, "let one interpret" is a key to understanding this section. When translated emphatically as in the

NASB it appears to suggest that Paul expected *one* individual to interpret the message of the two or three tongues speakers. Are we then to assume that a single person with the gift of interpretation could interpret anyone's speech? There is nothing in this text or any other text for that matter that suggests that an interpreter was something of a universal translator for any tongues speech. Such a suggestion would have required further explanation by Paul.

This problem is alleviated by translating this phrase in an indefinite sense as "let someone interpret." Tongues then were not to be used unless *someone* interpreted. Even so we are left with some vital questions which must be answered in either case. How could the tongues speaker know when he began speaking that someone was present who could interpret? Was the interpreter well known to the church and therefore one who would be conspicuous by his presence or absence? Some scholars have indeed argued that if the interpreter is absent, the tongues speaker must remain silent that particular day. I find this suggestion difficult to imagine since the Corinthians had shown no desire to use any of their gifts for edification. The likelihood that Paul was simply reminding them to wait for the interpreter to be present seems most unlikely.

I do think that "let someone interpret" is the right meaning, but suggest that Paul gave here only a general principle which must be understood in light of his previous references to tongues plus interpretation (14:5, 13-16). Why should we assume that Paul was adding a new wrinkle to his previous clear and pointed directions for the tongue speaker? Paul expected the tongue speaker who was zealous to edify, to pray for and receive the gift of interpretation (14:13). Remember in 14:5 that the basic line of thought was that the tongues speaker himself would interpret. This would enable him to minister in a way that would edify the Christians and avoid the risk of offending the non-Christian. In the light of 14:5, 13-16 the suggestion that someone else would interpret seems unlikely or at best a rare exception. This would resolve a significant problem: how did the tongues speaker know an interpreter was present when he felt led to speak? The tongues speaker, who has the companion gift of interpretation, had immediate confidence because he himself would be the "someone" who interpreted the message to make it edifying.

Verse 28 would then indicate that the tongues speaker who is not an interpreter should remain silent in the church. Paul's prohibition was not aimed at prohibiting anyone from contributing to the edification of the assembly, it was directed at the spiritual who was seeking to arrogantly display his "sign" gift. Even he had the freedom to speak to himself (14:4) and to God (14:2). He could practice his gift in private without speaking aloud in the assembly. It is unlikely that Paul was encouraging the tongues speaker to pray to himself in tongues while someone else was speaking. He could practice his gift at home, or perhaps silently in a moment of meditation during the worship service.

If we take into account what Paul had just described as the effect of tongues on the unbeliever (14:23), we must further suggest that Paul anticipated that the tongues speaker would receive his message as he prayed silently in the spirit and then deliver his interpreted message *audibly* through rational speech. I think that is the obvious implication of verse 15 followed by the warning of verse 23. The context and the historical situation both argue in favor of this interpretation. The risk of offending the unbelievers would lead the spiritual person to forfeit this right to speak audibly in tongues.

When teaching this, I have had people object that this is not how it has been practiced in charismatic churches. We cannot allow traditional practices, be they charismatic, Baptist, or whatever, to dictate our interpretation of Scripture. Perhaps our traditional practice has emerged because of an inadequate understanding of this passage. One further objection I have heard voiced is that this interpretation does not give the tongues speaker the freedom to practice this gift. On the contrary, the person is free to give the message which edifies. This is the goal of the truly spiritual person. As a spiritual person, he voluntarily gives up the right to use the gift audibly since it may well be a deterrent to the gospel (see 9:19).

I have also been asked whether the tongues speaker could tell the congregation that he/she received the message in a tongue. Again my response is to ask, What would be the purpose of such a statement? Does that statement edify the believers or draw attention to the speaker and the gift possessed? Gifts have one purpose and one value only when used in the assembly—the common good. I can see no way that such a statement would serve the common good given the mystery that surrounds this gift then and now.

Let's illustrate this concern in another way. Suppose each Sunday as I stood to preach I began with a detailed description of my preparation during the past week. "I want you to know that I spent eight hours in prayer and another ten hours researching and writing the sermon. I read five commentaries and checked out all the Greek tenses of the verbs. Now let me tell you the message God gave me for the church." Would you be able to hear God's message or would your attention be drawn to me as the recipient of the message? Anything that draws attention to the speaker and away from the message is irrelevant and must be discarded as spiritual egotism.

Paul's treatment of prophecy suggests that his concept of prophecy differed substantially from that of the spirituals. This manifestation too had been abused in Corinth, and therefore Paul limited the prophetic utterances at any one service to two or three. The implicit suggestion was that a prophet could exercise volitional control over his gift (see v. 32). Theoretically it may be necessary for him to leave without the opportunity to speak.

The statement "and let the *others* pass judgment" (v. 29) could refer to other prophets, or other believers or others with the gift of distinguishing spirits. In favor of "other believers" we should note that Paul taught that all Christians were responsible for evaluating prophetic utterances and determining whether they were good or bad (1 Thess. 5:19 *ff.;* 1 Cor. 2:13 *ff.;* and see 1 John 4:1). Yet there are others who argue convincingly that Paul had in mind here the function of those with a special gift for "distinguishing of spirits" (1 Cor. 12:10). A colleague of mine in England, James D.G. Dunn in his excellent book *Jesus and the Spirit* argues that "distinguishing of spirits" refers to the ability to evaluate both the source and content of prophetic utterance.[5]

It is obvious how many interpreters could be led to see such a gift in practice in this passage. Yet we are surprised that Paul would not simply say "the others with the gift for distinguishing spirits," if indeed he had that in mind.

Thus our decision on "the others" must be made based on the present context. It is apparent that Paul quite clearly turned his attention specifically to the functions of the prophets in verse 29. "The others" would most naturally refer to the other prophets who were not among the two or three who have the opportunity to speak. In verse 30 "another" (same Greek word) is repeated where it is certain that another prophet is in mind.

Still we have not answered the question: How do the prophets pass judgment? There are two interrelated issues which are vital to the proper understanding of this section. How is verse 29 related to verse 30 and why did Paul instruct the first prophet to be silent when interrupted, rather than asking the second to wait until the first had completed his message? In his insistence that the first prophet be silent, Paul differed greatly from the regulation of Qumran, 1 QL VI, 10: "One shall not speak in the midst of the words of his neighbor before his brother had finished speaking."[6] (Qumran was a community of Jews who, after a quarrel with the priesthood of Jerusalem, made a home for themselves near the Dead Sea.) This regulation is most surprising to the modern-day reader. Most of us were raised with the injunction that you don't interrupt when someone else is speaking. It would be rude.

The unexpected nature of this regulation has caused some to argue that Paul meant that the first prophet be silent once he had finished speaking. That is special pleading which goes against the tenor of the passage. Are we to think then that the prophetic speech is fragmentary so that the second prophet completes the message of the first? Is it that the fresher revelation is purer than the first? Should we conclude that when a prophet is inspired he cannot postpone the giving of his message, that he must have the freedom to speak whenever moved even if he were to interrupt another prophet? If we interpret verses 29-30 as closely related, then we can see that in verse 30 Paul gave a second level of control which could be exercised when a prophet failed to exercise self-restraint. The second prophet, the one interrupting, was one of "the others" who were evaluating the prophetic message. The Holy Spirit through the interruption of the second prophet judges that the first prophet was speaking without inspiration or by inspiration other than the Holy Spirit. Notice that two elements of control should always be at work in the assembly. The truly spiritual person will volitionally control his impluse to speak: but, if he fails to do so, divine control can be exercised by others who have authority to silence the speaker. One suspects again that this regulation was directed at the spirituals who wanted only to exhibit their gifts, not to edify the body.

We can draw a similar parallel from the life of the church today. Our church has a special Thanksgiving Day service where we place microphones throughout the church and invite people to give a short testimony of thanksgiving. Generally this moves along without a hitch. There have been some moments of deep stirring of the Spirit as people testify to the working of God in their lives. Occasionally we have had someone approach the microphone to share a thanksgiving testimony and then they continued on to lecture the church concerning some failing or to draw attention to their own ministry within the church. As I have watched the faces of the listeners from the vantage point of the pulpit, I could visibly see the uneasiness when it became apparent that the speaker had exceeded his/her inspiration. There have been times that I have felt it necessary to intervene and say, "Thank you, we must allow someone else to share now." This experience is not unlike the regulation being placed upon the prophets.

After this brief aside to discuss the task of "the others" who were judging the prophets, Paul took up the specific matter of orderly prophetic speech. All those with a prophetic gift could employ their gifts "one by one" (v. 31) so the whole body may learn and be encouraged. There is an implicit relationship between the orderly use of prophetic gifts and the positive results witnessed in the church.

The phrase "the spirits of the prophets are subject to the prophets" has elicited much discussion. Two major lines of interpretation have emerged: (1) The "spirits" of the prophets are subjected to the rational control of the prophets themselves. The emphasis in this case is on the prophet controlling himself. The plural "spirits" have been variously taken to mean "prophetic gifts," "revelations and inspirations," or "human spirits." As we previously noted, volitional control would be necessary for the prophet to obey the regulations concerning the number of speakers and the orderly sequence. The ability to control one's gift seems to be assumed throughout chapter 12. 2) A second line of interpretation argues that the "spirits" of the prophets are subject to other prophets, that is to the discernment of the other prophets who are listening. As we have seen, Paul did allow for outside control when the rational or volitional control was ignored and unseemly behavior resulted. This external control was clearly in view in verse 30. Since both ideas find support from the context, it may well be that Paul used the plural "spirits" in an ambivalent manner to suggest both of these elements of control which were to be present in every assembly.

In either case you should notice that this section on the ordering of the worship service was sealed by an appeal to the very nature of God. "God is not a God of confusion but of peace." I would suspect that if one had viewed the Corinthian worship service with its uncontrolled exercise of gifts, one may not have surmised that the God of these people was orderly. The proper exercise of *charismata* will always bear witness to the presence (14:25) and nature of God (v. 33). The unbridled exercise of gifts by the spirituals had not borne such testimony.

I have had people object to this interpretation on the basis that they cannot control their urge to speak or to burst forth in tongues. This passage gives no encouragement for the argument that one cannot control the exercise of gifts. First, God places the gifts under the rational control of the believer. If the believer fails to exercise control, there are those in the assembly who may call them to be silent.

Let the Women Keep Silent

Not many phrases have created as much interest as "Let the women keep silent in the churches." It has created interest both in terms of its relationship to the preceding discussion and its apparent "contradiction" to the teaching of 1 Corinthians 11. Some scholars have therefore suggested that this was not a part of the original text, but was added later by another author. The evidence from early manuscripts does not support this suggestion, and when rightly interpreted there is no contradiction with the content of 1 Corinthians 11.

I cannot indulge in a detailed treatment of 1 Corinthians 11, but I should like to consider it in relation to this present context. Paul first addressed the matter of women participating in the worship service in 11:2-16, a section which is obscure because of the references to traditions and customs which are difficult to reconstruct. There have been numerous suggestions concerning the meaning of the covering of the woman's head. Whether one thinks that the head covering is a veil, a specific hairstyle, or a positive symbol of authority, the obvious implication was that a woman may pray and prophesy if she conformed to the custom held by all the churches of God (11:16). If, however, she behaved contentiously, "we have no other practice, nor have the churches of God."

Within certain stipulations of custom, Paul allowed a woman to exercise prophecy in the assembly if she was led by the Spirit of God to do so. Theoretically, we would be led to conclude that a woman might receive and utilize any gift which the Spirit gives as *He* wills. Paul's teaching on the recipients of gifts was general, emphasizing only that *all the members* of the body received gifts and might exercise them in the church for the edification of the body. Passages such as Romans 16, 1 Corinthians 16:19, and Philippians 4:2-3 suggest that Paul held a high view of the ministry of women. Perhaps he did so because of his understanding of the working of the Spirit through the gifts.

Can we reconcile the approval of 11:5 and the prohibition of 14:34 without a forced harmonization? Some scholars have suggested that these two passages belong to different letters, but even that does not soften the contrast. The attempt of other teachers to explain chapter 11 in terms of a prayer meeting in a home and not in the gathered assembly is unconvincing. We would do well to recall that the early church had no church buildings and they regularly met from house to house.

Some argue that Paul was prohibiting women from speaking in tongues in 14:34, but this is not evident from 14:34-35 itself, nor was the immediate context about tongues. It was about prophecy. Presumably, if Paul would permit women to prophesy, he would allow them to share a message transmitted in a tongue if inspired to do so. The most popular view is that Paul here was prohibiting the women from questioning and judging the prophets. J. Hurley, for example, thinks this was prohibited by the divinely ordained structure of authority.[7] A woman would be required then to usurp the authority of man. While this seems at first appealing, it is not fully satisfactory. Could a woman respond to the prophecy of another woman? Remember Paul allowed a woman to prophesy in chapter 11. More importantly, could a woman with the gift of prophecy or the "discerning of spirits" speak in response to a man if prompted by the Spirit?

These logical problems have led some to say that Paul acknowledged the principle of equality in the Christian life in chapter 11 but was unwilling to implement it.[8] In that case B. Hall's accusation that this was one of Paul's worst moments in which he had forgotten the implications of Galatians 3:28 is not strong enough. He had also ignored his teaching in a preceding chapter.[9] It is difficult to imagine that Paul, who had been so careful in his argument up to this point, would so blatantly contradict himself. It also strikes at one's view of inspiration to suggest that Paul could contradict himself writing under the direction of the Holy Spirit.

I believe we can answer these difficult questions by paying careful attention to both the historical and immediate context. Don't lose sight of the fact that the command to keep silent was repeated three times. He told the tongues speaker who did not interpret to keep silent. He instructed the prophet interrupted by a second prophet to keep silent. I have suggested that in the first two instances Paul had in mind the spirituals who had no concern for edification. Is it possible that "Let the women keep silent in the churches" (notice the plural) had in view the silencing of female spirituals who desired to participate in the service with little regard to traditions or the good of others? Their only desire was to display their freedom! You might object that in the case of the women there is no evidence that Paul had in mind any exceptions, whereas the exceptions were stated in regard to the tongues speaker and prophet. This objection overlooks a central point. The control of the tongues speaker and the prophet was dealt with only in chapter 14, whereas the participation of the women in the assembly is dealt with in two separate chapters. It might be added that the instructions of verses 27-28 concerning tongues speech depend on the earlier discussion in verses 13-16 for clarity. In the case of the women, the exception which allowed women to speak in the assembly, emerges clearly when the two passages concerned with this matter are taken together.

Paul intentionally introduced this discussion of women speaking with the phrase "as in all the churches of the saints" (33*b*) in order to remind the readers of his previous instructions allowing women to speak under certain conditions (ch. 11). Notice that the discussion was concluded with the reminder, "We have no other practice, nor have the churches of God." Rather than repeating the complex instructions given in chapter 11, Paul simply called them to mind with a similar phrase concerning church tradition. You are aware that the verse divisions are not original to the text. The phrase "as in all the churches of the saints" has more meaning when taken with verse 34 as an introduction rather than being tagged onto verse 33 as an ending to the former discussion. Notice that Paul widens the scope of the discussion concerning worship to the practice in all the churches (plural). This is a third element of control concerning the abusive and confusing use of gifts for wrong purposes. Each denomination might do well to ponder how this fits into its own denominational structure.

The general expressions "speak" and "speak in the church" are given content by the words *learn* and *ask*. The contentious behavior Paul had in mind here was that of women who demanded their right to prophesy without any regard for tradition. It could also refer to speaking that included an arrogant debating and questioning that was creating a disgraceful confusion. Therefore Paul did not intend to rescind the permission to speak given in chapter 11, he desired only to silence the women spirituals who behaved shamefully. They had thrown off all restrictions of decency and order under the banner of freedom, because of their desire to prove their spirituality. They, like the tongues speaker who could not interpret and the prophet who was interrupted, must be silent in the church.

I would point out one other factor linking chapters 11 and 14 together. The problem in chapter 11 is intricately bound to a woman praying or prophesying with her head uncovered. This is a notoriously difficult text because of our uncertainty about head coverings in the time of Jesus. It seems that the issue was concerning the wearing of the hair as a covering. The Jewish woman would wear her hair tightly braided on top of her head as a covering (11:15). When a woman let her hair down in public, she was making a sexual statement. I often tell people it is reminiscent of the words of the country song, that when she lets her hair down, it's behind closed doors. Was not this the reaction of the Pharisees when the woman wiped Jesus' feet with her hair? They exclaimed, "If this man were a prophet He would know who and what sort of person this woman is who is touching Him, that she is a sinner" (Luke 7:39). Was their information based on a personal knowledge or the obvious clue that she had her hair down in public?

We can attempt to reconstruct the scene. Can you imagine the difficulty early Christians had, particularly Jewish Christians, when women were introduced in to the worship service where there was neither male or female? In the Temple they had been relegated to the court of the women while in the synagogue they stood outside. To worship together was hard enough! Now you tell me that they have the right to pray and prophesy. Let me have a little while to digest this new idea. Just when I have come to grips with this second difficult truth, the woman beside me stands to prophesy. She dramatically pulls the combs from her unshorn hair and it falls across my lap. Culture shock is one thing—this is too much!

Her dramatic statement brought dishonor to her *head*. There is a play on words. She disgraced her own head by wearing her hair like a prostitute. If that is what she is she should have her head shaved (11:6). Likely this was the punishment for an adulteress. But she had also brought dishonor upon her husband (also her head). She had, by this dramatic statement, declared herself sexually available and thus disgraced him. It was therefore fitting that in 14:33 when Paul reminded them of this particular occasion, he subjected the woman to her husband's authority. She had dishonored him and now she must be subjected to him.

Admittedly both passages are difficult. It is apparent that Paul was not suggesting that a woman should not participate in discussion for the sake of learning. It is also obvious that he would not contradict the obvious teaching of chapter 11. If you find the suggestion I have offered as overly subtle, we are left with a final but dissatisfying solution. We must simply say the events cannot be reconstructed with enough clarity to fully understand the problem in Corinth related to women. We must then assume that the Corinthians who were well aware of their own daily problems had enough background to distinguish between the prohibition of this section and the approval of chapter 11.

These Are the Lord's Commandments

The concluding verses of chapter 14 again remind us of the background for understanding Paul's ordering and regulating the service of worship. Verse 36 is an ironic reference to the extravagant behavior of the spirituals who were behaving as if the gospel had originated with them or as if they alone were Christians. Their individualistic behavior reflected their arrogant claim to be spirituals and had led to confusion in worship as well as everyday affairs. There was also the reminder that they were not alone in the Christian faith. Not only must they be concerned for the other brethren in Corinth, but for the wider fellowship of believers. There were certain traditions which must be maintained by all the churches of God (see 1:2; 11:2,16; 14:34,36; and 16:1).

Because spiritual manifestations and persons are at the very heart of the Corinthian difficulties, it is altogether fitting that Paul's strongest warning was given after the full teaching concerning the gifts had been completed. Paul was doubtless aware that some might have been tempted to refute his teaching either on the basis of his lack of spiritual manifestations or on the basis of their own superior knowledge. But, as H. Chadwick has so perceptively pointed out, verses 37-38 are "a masterly sentence which has the effect of brilliantly forestalling possible counterattack at the most dangerous point, and indeed carries the war into the enemy camp."[10]

"If anyone thinks he is a prophet or spiritual" has a slightly ironical connotation. The spirituals entertained no doubt about their elevated status, but Paul attacked the very heart of their claims and established a new criterion for proving oneself a spiritual. Paul utilized both prophet and spiritual person for impact and comprehensiveness. Although the specific corrections in this chapter have been levelled against the spirituals, this conclusion has implications for all. All who accept the conditions of this teaching will show themselves truly spiritual.

Paul gave a specific answer to the question: "Don't the spiritual gifts prove we are the spiritual persons?" An individual will prove himself to be a spiritual person by acknowledging that these things which are written are the commands of the Lord. Thus we are brought again to our two criteria: discernment of the "graciousness" of Christian existence and the resulting fruit behavior characterized by love.

Paul's use of "the Lord's commandments" has been troublesome to many interpreters. In 1 Corinthians 7:10 Paul indicated that his statement concerning divorce was the Lord's command. In that context he almost certainly was making reference to the actual teaching of the earthly Jesus. In 11:23 Paul referred to a verbal tradition which had been received from the Lord and handed down by others (cf. 15:3). It is highly unlikely that Paul was appealing here to an actual word of Jesus or for that matter to any previously written material. Paul here brought to bear the full weight of his own apostolic authority. We have a similar occurrence in Romans 15:15, although the point was not so drastically stated in that case. Paul insisted therefore that these directions be obeyed with the same fidelity with which one would obey a command of the Lord. Considering the care with which Paul distinguished between the actual words of the Lord and his own opinion, one is indeed impressed with the strength of this statement.

There is a tendency to underplay the severity of verse 35. It should be recalled that Paul began this section: "Now concerning spiritual gifts, brethren, I do not want you to be unaware" (*agnoeō*). Now that Paul had fully discussed both the spiritual gifts and spiritual persons, he placed before them the standard by which they must judge themselves. If they fail to comprehend the nature of the grace gifts and to utilize their gifts for edification, they will demonstrate that they are not spiritual persons. It is not that they will remain ignorant concerning gifts, but they will not be recognized by God (see 8:1-3). They will prove themselves to be spiritual imposters. It is for this very reason that Paul could boldly prohibit their speaking in the assembly.

Paul concluded with a brief but positive summation: They should zealously desire prophecy (14:1,12), and tongues should not be forbidden. The contrast between Paul's enthusiasm for the one and his provisional acceptance of the other is reminiscent of chapter 14. This again was based on his concern for edification. "But let all things be done properly and in an orderly manner."

It is frequently argued regarding chapter 14 that Paul established a "charismatic" order for worship, and therefore he knew of *no leader* to whom he could appeal in order to achieve ordered worship. The first statement is somewhat exaggerated, and the subsequent conclusion is totally unwarranted. Paul did set forth regulations whereby one gifted member might control another in the assembly, but this must be kept in historical perspective. Given the attitude of the spirituals toward tradition and those they considered to be nonspirituals (leaders), an appeal by Paul for Stephanas or Achaicus to order the worship service would have been ill conceived. The spirituals would have rejected that because in their estimation they lacked gifts. As with so many issues in this letter, Paul established an order for the worship service which was based on criteria which the spirituals logically could not reject. They no doubt would object to what they considered an artificial limitation of their spiritual activity, but what objection could they raise to "charismatic" control which was based on the very *nature of God who is the Author of the gifts?* As was previously argued, 14:26 *ff.* provided a firm control for silencing the individual who was not concerned to edify. For example, the prophet, redefined as one who speaks for purposes of edification, exhortation, and consolation, can interrupt and silence the prophet who is judged to be speaking without inspiration. There are also regulations concerning the number of speakers and orderliness which Paul established and declared inviolable. Finally, it should be noted that Paul did in fact tell the Corinthians that they must be in subjection to men like Stephanas and all those who help in the work and labor (16:16). The fact that Paul did not specifically appeal to Stephanas or Achaicus to control the assembly does not mean that he could not have done so were the situation amendable to such a solution. It seems probable that they were among those gifted as prophets and teachers.

Drawing Together Our Thoughts

(1) Spiritual manifestations (*pnuematika*), sought immaturely and individualistically for their sign value, were at the heart of the Corinthian difficulties. The *pneumatika* of Corinth were primarily the miraculous speech and knowledge gifts (1:4-7; 12:8-10; 13:1-3).

(2) Numerous factors were involved in the formulation of Paul's concept of the charismatic community, but the Corinthian situation provided the catalyst for its emergence and in many respects the shaping force for its expression. The expositor must always bear in mind that the concepts which we collectively refer to as Paul's "theology of spiritual gifts" were hammered out on the anvil of experience.

(3) The term *charisma* was selected as an appropriate designation for discussing the spiritual manifestations in 1 Corinthians because of (a) the exaggerated emphasis on spiritual gifts as a sign of the spiritual person and (b) the corrective of grace *(charis)* which was at the heart of the entire Corinthian letter and is therefore appropriately applied to the gifts. The emphasis is on God as the ultimate *Source of all gifts*

and thus forms a counterbalance to any semblance of arrogance concerning the possession of a particular gift.

(4) All believers are spiritual in the broadest sense of that term since the confession "Jesus is Lord" comes only by the Holy Spirit. All are baptized into the body by the one Spirit. Since God manifests His grace in the empowering of the community for service, all believers possess *charismata*. The baptism of the Holy Spirit, rightly understood, is the experience of salvation which incorporates us into the life of the body of Christ.

(5) All Christians are responsible functioning members of the community, and therefore the variety of gifts is necessary for unity, a concept forshadowed in 1 Thessalonians 5.

(6) The body imagery first emerged in Pauline teaching in 1 Corinthians, and it is likely that its specific formulation was related to the newly developed concept—"all members were empowered for unique functions in the community." The body imagery provided an obvious illustration to bring a necessary corrective.

(7) Although all are gifted and responsible for ministry, there is a divinely ordained structure of leadership. These persons too are gifted and believers must be subject to those who function in such leadership roles (also foreshadowed in 1 Thess. 5).

(8) *Gifts* and *behavior* were closely interwoven in 1 Corinthians, and this was largely owing to the divorce of such in Corinth. The authentically spiritual person was redefined as one whose life is controlled by love, the greatest expression of the eternal in the now. Grace gifts provide for the spiritual person, not a source of boasting, but a means for expressing love, experienced in the assembly (*ekklesia*) in terms of edification.

(9) An understanding of those things which were considered by Paul to be *charismata* is best gained by attention to Paul's lists, especially 1 Corinthians 12:28, where Paul intentionally broadens the "gift" concept to include leadership and routine service abilities. The suggestions that *charismata* are only "activities of the moment" or

that they are heightened natural abilities are both too narrow. On the other hand the idea that anything done for the good of the body becomes *charismata* is too broad. Paul had in mind abilities, both transitory and permanent, miraculous and routine, which enable one to function as a member of the body. These must be recognized as "the things freely given to us by God" (2:12) and utilized in the power of the Spirit for the *common good*. We will return to deal with the question—Is there a specific number of gifts?—later in our study.

(10) The redefined spiritual person whose concern is for the edification of the body will seek to abound for the edification of the church. This will affect both his desire for certain gifts and the use of any gift that person might possess.

(11) The specific directions concerning the control of gifts in chapter 14 were made necessary by the Corinthian abuses, and thus universalizing applications must be made with some caution. The control of gifts was twofold: volitional and external. The spiritual person, who was concerned for the edification of the church, can and will control his gift. External control is accomplished as the Spirit controls one individual by means of another. The instructions of Paul in 14:26 *ff.* and the interruption of the first prophet by the second are two examples. A third, but less emphasized control, is the tradition of customs shared by the larger Christian community.

(12) Three special features should be noted: (a) The instructions concerning "gifts" are basic and comprehensive; (b) Paul was suspect to the spirituals because of his apparent lack of miraculous gifts; (c) Paul's boast that he himself possessed an abundant gift of tongues would have had its desired effect only if it came as a surprise to the readers. Together these things suggest that Paul did not introduce the miraculous gifts to the Corinthians. He thus wrote 1 Corinthians in response to a query concerning difficulties which had developed after his departure.

(13) Paul did not deny the value of ecstatic religious phenomena, but he greatly preferred that intelligible gifts be used in the assembly.

Paul tentatively and diplomatically made a place for tongues in the Corinthian assembly, but apparently preferred that tongues be practiced privately owing to their inherent limitations. Tongues should not be spoken publicly because they could become a deterrent to the advance of the gospel. The tongues speaker who desired to edify through the gift of tongues should pray for the gift of interpretation. The message would be received as the tongues speaker prayed in the Spirit and then transmitted verbally in a language all could understand.

(14) Since the teaching in 1 Corinthians was first aimed at correcting the aberration of the spirituals we must look closely at writings that occur after this letter to determine what *thoughts* Paul carried forward when he was not correcting Corinthian misunderstanding.

Notes

1. See later in 14:28 when speaking to God silently is a positive alternative to speaking in the assembly.

2. G. G. Findlay, *St. Paul's First Epistle to the Corinthians,* (London: Hodder and Stoughton, 1900), p. 902. See also R. N. Longenecker, *Paul: Apostle of Liberty,* (New York: Harper and Row, Publishers, 1964), p. 45.

3. It is difficult to assess the nature of New Testament manifestations of tongues. E. Best illustrates the difficulty of making decisions about the nature of New Testament and contemporary tongues-speaking practices in "The Interpretation of Tongues," *Scottish Journal of Theology,* vol. 28 (1975), pp. 45-62. This is not a major concern of this book but see the comments under 13:1, 14:13-16, 27-28.

4. It may be argued that the separate listing of tongues and interpretation in 12:10,30: and 14:26 dictate against the view given here. However, the separate listing does not necessarily conflict with the thrust of my argument. While "interpretation" might be employed by a person different from the tongues speaker, that would be an exception rather than the rule. The specific directions of chapter 14 must be given more weight for answering this question than the listings of chapter 12 where this issue was not in mind.

5. James D. G. Dunn, *Jesus and the Spirit,* (London, 1975, SCM Press, Ltd.) pp. 233 *ff.*

6. H. Braun, *Qumran und das Neue Testament* (2 vols.) (Tubingen: J. C. B. Mohr, 1966), I 196.

7. J. B. Hurley, "Did Paul Require Veils or the Silence of Woman? A Consideration

of 1 Cor. 11:2-16 and 1 Cor. 14: 33b-36," *Westminister Theological Journal,* vol. 35 (1973), pp. 190-220.

8. P. K. Jewett, *Man as Male and Female* (Grand Rapids: Wm. B. Eerdmans, 1975), p 111 *ff.*

9. B. Hall, "Paul and Women," *Theology Today,* vol. 31 (1974), p. 55.

10. H. Chadwick, "All Things to All Men," *New Testament Studies,* (1955), p. 269.

6
Rome, a Control Situation

I was never much of a science student during my high-school or college years, but a few simple things did stick. If you are planning an experiment you need to have a control situation, so you can determine what caused the actual results of your experiment. We are familiar with the claims of various toothpaste companies to reduce cavities. In order to verify their results they must have a control group who used brand X or their own toothpaste with the key ingredients missing. They then report the results: those using our brand with our secret ingredient had 35 percent fewer cavities. I've often wondered how those folks in the other control group with a mouth full of cavities felt.

If we are attempting to discover the essential elements in Pauline teaching concerning spiritual gifts, it would be nice to have a control community—a community that Paul had not visited and thus had not taught, a community that was not already struggling with numerous problems concerning spiritual gifts. In such a situation what would Paul write? In many ways Romans gives us this control situation.

The Writing of Romans

Most scholars agree that Paul wrote Romans after 1 Corinthians, probably from Corinth during the three-month period described in Acts 20:2 *ff.* However, the occasion of the letter and the related questions concerning Paul's specific knowledge of the Roman community are debatable issues. Numerous theories have been advanced, but they can be summarized under three broad categories.

129

Few modern scholars would call Romans a theological treatise, but many would argue that its comprehensive content, systematic structure and general tone clearly distinguish it from other Pauline Epistles. Consequently, many scholars conclude that Romans reflects a concrete historical situation, but that it was primarily Paul's personal situation. Therefore, they argue that Romans tells us little or nothing about the conditions in Rome. Paul, at the time of the writing, had just emerged from painful community problems in Galatia, Corinth, and Macedonia. Having worked through several issues in the heat of controversy, he now took the opportunity to give his mature and considered judgment on these matters in a systematic fashion and with universal application. You have no doubt already wondered, *Why would Paul write a general letter reflecting his own situation to Rome, a church unknown to him?* This has occurred to other readers and has been answered several ways, but most creatively in the suggestion that Romans was originally a circular letter. No doubt Paul's struggles of the recent past are reflected in chapters 1—11 and probably in chapters 12—15, and the significance of his approaching trip is specifically mentioned (15:25 *ff.*). It is doubtful whether this alone accounts for the content and writing of Romans, nor does it take seriously enough Paul's pastoral interest in the Roman Christians (1:9-11; 15:15, 24).

Second, it is frequently suggested that the primary motive in the writing of Romans was missionary. Paul desired to share with the Romans in order to win them for his gospel and thus to solicit their support for the expansion of his ministry into Spain (1:10-15 and 15:22-29). This view has the obvious advantage of taking Paul's expressed intent for writing at face value, and it helps to explain the inclusion of the detailed description of Paul's ministry and gospel in chapters 1—11. However, this does not fully account for the specific admonitions in chapters 14—15.

There have been several attempts, not all of them recent, to reconstruct a specific situation in Rome to which Paul was addressing himself. Characteristically these reconstructions center around the identification of the "weak" and the "strong" mentioned in chapters

14—15. Nevertheless, there is considerable disagreement concerning the precise nature of the tension. Some scholars locate the difficulties in the Jewish Christians, but most commentators find the "strong" Gentiles more at fault. H.W. Bartsch boldly suggested that the Gentiles despised the Jews as barbarians and as weak in the faith and that the hostility was so intense that no church had been established in Rome.[1] Paul Minear similarly found no church, but discovered instead five distinct factions.[2] Still others found in Rome a libertine or Gnostic faction similar to that of Corinth. The evidence for Paul's knowledge of such a serious problem is indeed slight, and one must ask whether Paul would oppose such problems with tenacity in Corinth or Galatia and then respond so passively in Romans. Perhaps those finding a Judaizing or a libertine faction are hearing too strongly the echo of past difficulties. Conspicious also are the positive references to the faith of the Romans (Rom. 1:8-15; 15:12,24).

Such elaborate reconstructions in regard to the Roman letter rely more on the ingenuity of the scholar than concrete evidence. Romans simply does not yield such a complete picture. Nevertheless, it is likely that there is an element of truth in all the aforementioned approaches. Paul apparently had some knowledge of the local situation (1:9; 15:-14), and his pastoral concern for the Romans must not go unheeded. It is not unreasonable to think that Paul, desirous as he was to visit Rome (1:10-15), would have gathered information concerning the condition of Christianity there. Paul knew several members of the Roman community (Rom. 16). It is conceivable that someone like Aquila and Priscilla could have provided rather detailed information.

The discussion of chapters 12—15 may well have been prompted by knowledge of Roman difficulties, but even so the full discussion may actually reflect Paul's recent controversies more than it does the actual Roman situation. It is equally apparent that Paul's attention in this letter is often focused on himself; his coming trip to Jerusalem and mission work in Spain. This is so prominent that even when Paul specifically addresses the Romans concerning his confidence in them and his apology for writing so boldly, he moved immediately to a discussion of his own special ministry (15:14 *ff.*).

A Gift Problem in Rome

If we grant that Paul had some knowledge of the Roman community, we are faced with a question even more central to our enquiry. Does Romans 12 reflect a unique historical situation? Was Paul aware of a problem concerning "spiritual gifts" in Rome? Chrysostom, in the Fourth century, commenting on 1 Corinthians 12:1-2, mentioned that the Romans were having problems related to "gifts," but not so seriously as were the Corinthians. Chrysostom's suggestion was apparently based on the assumption that this was a universal problem, and he confessed that the whole matter was obscure since the spiritual manifestations had ceased.[3] While there are a few modern scholars who suggest that Paul may have been aware of Corinthian-like gift problems in Rome, they are not very convincing. I would raise several general objections to such an assumption.

(1) The letter as a whole betrays no misunderstanding like those in Corinth. You can simply contrast the tone of the two letters. (2) The brevity of the gift passage would be surprising if Paul were aware of this type of problem. (3) More surprising, however, would be the nonspecific nature of the passage. The content is more in the form of general principles than corrective exhortation. The specific gifts mentioned certainly betray no such problems, and the ethical teaching in 12:9 *ff.* is more general than 1 Corinthians 13.

If Romans 12 does not clearly reflect a Roman situation, what is the value of this passage for our enquiry? Being "nonsituational" the passage is neutral, and thus it can function like a "control" in a scientific experiment. Nevertheless, it must be remembered that no passage is entirely neutral. First, Paul's own situation, particularly the recent Corinthian situation, must be kept in mind. Second, although Paul's motive for writing Romans was multifaceted, one explicit purpose, attested to both by the existence of the letter (15:15) and by verses such as Romans 1:5-6, 8-15, and 15:24, was that it might benefit the Romans. Therefore, it is likely that one discovers in this gift passage important truths concerning community ministry which Paul thought would benefit them.

There are several important questions which must be considered. If, as I suggest, the Corinthian situation elicited and, in some sense, shaped Paul's thought on the functioning of the gifted body, were the insights developed in that passage in response to a "spiritual" aberration still maintained in this less-situational setting? Were they somewhat more developed, or was the emphasis altered? Why did Paul include a gift passage if he had little information about Rome and possibly none about the structure of community ministry? Did Paul summarize those principles which he believed to be at the heart of his "gift teaching" and which therefore should be shared with every community, even one he had not founded? If this passage can shed light on any of these issues, it will prove to be of considerable importance.

The Context of Romans 12

The division between theological teaching and application is more obviously pronounced in Romans than in most of the other Pauline letters. Romans chapters 1—11 are basically theological in content, whereas chapters 12—15 are ethical teaching. While the break is rather obvious, there is every indication that the teaching material is related to and dependent on the theological formulation in chapters 1—11. The content of these two sections is tied closely together by the phrase, "I urge you therefore, brethren, by the mercies of God" (12:1). The admonitions of chapters 12—15 are based on the truth that the brethren had received God's mercies which were described in chapters 1-11.

Romans 12:1-2 forms a prelude for the teaching which will follow. The presentation of the body and the transformation by the renewal of the mind are the bases upon which the following exhortation is constructed. This is important for our study because it demonstrates that the foundation for the discussion of *charisma* in Romans is the *graciousness* of God experienced in personal relationship. Remember that 1 Corinthians 12:1-3 played precisely that role in the Corinthian correspondence. Numerous commentators have attempted to explain the progression of thought in chapter 12. Some have questioned whether there is any logical progression. It is important to note that verses 3-8 deal with the ministering community while verses 9-14 deal with the daily life in community. I would call specific attention to the observation that the progression of thought from verses 3-8 to verses 9-14 can be compared to the progression from 1 Corinthians 12 to 1 Corinthians 13.

Yet this comparison of Romans 12:3-14 with 1 Corinthians 12—13 obscures the rather curious fact that the actual discussion of gifts in Romans 12:3-8 is surrounded by ethical instruction. In fact, the teaching on gifts somewhat interrupts the ethical teaching. The concluding phrase of verse 2, "that which is good and acceptable and perfect," prepares the reader for a discussion of ethical behavior. Yet this phrase is followed by a call for sober evaluation and proper utilization of the gifts for ministry. Consequently the pattern in Romans 12 is actually a reversal of 1 Corinthians 12—14 where the specifically ethical discussion came in the middle of the gift discussion (ch. 13). At this point I would only draw attention to this fact to underline the specific location of the discussion of gifts in Romans 12. Any suggestions concerning the significance of this structure must await our consideration of the passage.

Understanding the Prelude

Since verses 1-2 serve as a bridge and a prelude, it is necessary to look briefly at their significance. Paul began this teaching section with the exhortation: "Present your bodies . . . to God." "Present" or "place at one's disposal" is here linked with "sacrifice" and therefore takes on a sacrificial meaning. In contrast to "dead" animal sacrifices of the Old Testament era. Christians must present their bodies to God as living sacrifices. Most commentators assign to *body* a broad significance, such as the totality of the personality or one's capacity for communication. The impact of this passage is enhanced if the physical meaning of body is maintained.

The three qualifying words "living," "holy," and "acceptable" are of equal value. The Christian sacrifice is "living," not only in contrast to dead animal sacrifices, but in a theological sense. That is, the believer has been granted newness of life (Rom. 6:4 and see 8:6,11) and can therefore consider himself to be alive to God in Christ Jesus (6:11). It is only natural that those who have been made alive in Christ should present themselves as alive from the dead and their members as instruments of righteousness to God. The body as "living" sacrifice must continually be presented to God in selfless service. Our bodies are a continuous sacrifice that have been provided for us by God Himself.

"Holy" underlines both the totality of the sacrifice and its ethical character. The Christian's body is placed at God's disposal, and therefore the Christian who is "sacrificed" no longer lays claim to himself (see 1 Cor. 6:19-20). The sacrifice is "holy" in an ethical sense, corresponding to the nature of God. This living and holy sacrifice is that which is acceptable in the sense that it is what God requires and only that which He will accept. Anything less is insufficient (see Rom. 14:18).

A proper understanding of this principle of living sacrifice would solve the problems we confront in the church today from lack of commitment. A living sacrifice no longer has claim over time, money, and so forth. Once we have given ourselves bodily to God we no longer have to struggle with uncommitted areas of our lives. Many Christians want to pick and choose their areas of sacrifice—I'll do this but I won't do that. Living sacrifice means total commitment that responds, "Speak Lord for Thy servant hears."

The last phrase of verse 1 is difficult to translate. The Greek word is *logikos* and can be translated as "spiritual" or "reasonable." The phrase modifies "Present your bodies . . . to God," and it is clear that the presentation of the body is the basis for Christian service. *Logikos* is not to be taken as "spiritual" as if the contrast were between the internal New Testament worship and the external Old Testament sacrificial system. There is a contrast here with the sacrificial worship of the Old Testament, but it is secondary. The emphasis on *body* is difficult to understand if Paul desired only to indicate the inwardness of Christian worship.

I think that the translation "rational" is better, but not in the sense that it is worship of the "mind and heart" (NEB), but in the sense of "appropriate to" or "logical." The worship which is "appropriate to" the nature of Christian existence, which has been described in chapters 1—11, is the presentation of the body for service. Paul made a similar emphasis in 1 Corinthians 6:20, "For you have been brought with a price: therefore glorify God in your body." Thus the phrase "logical service" called to mind the content of Romans 6:13. If God has made our very bodies as alive from the dead through the gift of His Son, what else other than our bodies could we give Him as an appropriate act of worship? The remainder of this chapter is a description of the *practical outworking* of appropriate Christian worship based on living sacrifice. Notice that Paul first applied this principle of proper worship to the functioning of the gifted community.

Although Christian worship takes place in a real-world situation, the Christian cannot permit himself to be conformed to the values of the present age. The believer has victory over the tyrannizing forces of this age by submitting himself (6:12-13, 17-18,22; 8:5,13; see Gal. 5:16 *ff.*) to the transforming power of God. This power is active in the present age, and is here described as the constant "renewing of the mind" (RSV). Compare the thought of 2 Corinthians 3:18 and especially 4:16. "Mind" denotes the inner part of the constitution where feeling, thinking, and willing take place. It is not a matter of becoming more intelligent, but of the reorientation of thought and life to align with the truth experienced in Christ. The non-Christian mind is reprobate, issuing in a futile life-style (Rom. 1:28 *ff.*), but the Christian mind is constantly being renewed with the positive purpose of "proving" the will of God. "Prove" here means both the ability to discern and the power to embrace and verify the will of God in concrete activity. In the immediate context "proving the will of God" is first given ethical meaning, as is clearly indicated by the threefold qualification: good, acceptable, and perfect. The renewal begun in the believer by the Spirit will be evident in the behavior of the Christian (see Eph. 4:17-19,22-24; 5:8-10; Phil. 1:9-10; and esp. Col. 3).

Paul immediately followed the introductory frontispiece with a brief discussion of *charismata* instead of moving directly to the specific ethical instructions of verse 9 *ff.* This intrusion of the discussion of gifts into an ethical teaching context was intended to give proper perspective to the purpose and place of *charismata* within the larger scope of the Christian life. Second, Paul wanted to bring forward and apply to the discussion of gifts the two concepts of bodily "sacrifice" and "mind" renewal. The logical coherence of the passage demonstrates that Paul was very deliberate in developing the order of this section.

According to the *Grace* Given to Me

It is important to notice that Paul addressed the Romans "in virtue of" (Moffatt) the grace (*charis*) given him. In the present context this phrase was not intended to give apostolic authority to his appeal, but rather to underline Paul's dependence, in his apostolic ministry, on the empowering of God. This relationship between grace and Paul's ministry can best be demonstrated by looking at several passages in chronological sequence.

Paul stated in Galatians 2:8-9 that when the apostles saw that he had been entrusted with the gospel to the uncircumcised they acknowledged his apostolic ministry. Simply put, when the other apostles saw that God energized Paul's work as He did that of Peter, they were forced to recognize the grace that had been given him. Thus the grace (*charis*) given Paul was the energizing of God for the ministry to the Gentiles. The same concept is found in 1 Corinthians 3:10 where Paul discussed his specific ministry of founding churches and noted that he laid the foundation: "According to the grace [*charis*] of God which was given to me, as a wise master builder." In 1 Corinthians 15:10 Paul described his apostolic labors and declared: "But by the grace of God I am what I am," expressing his total dependence upon the enabling power of God. In that same passage he described this grace as an active force working through him in his apostolic labors. Romans 1:5 is most instructive because grace and apostleship are brought together by Paul. In the light of our previous examples, it appears that Paul was saying that he had received grace (*charis*), God's special energizing for his task, and the corresponding gift (*charisma*) in his apostleship. Therefore in Romans 12:3 and 15:15 Paul acknowledged that his apostolic ministry to them was the direct result of the grace which had been given him by God. Notice that grace takes on a sense beyond that of God's goodness in the forgiveness of sins. It also became the empowering force for ministry.

Notice that Paul repeated *charis* in similar phrases describing both his ministry and the ministry of the Romans: "through the grace given to me" (v. 3) and "according to the grace given to us" (v. 6). This repetition of *charis* forms an indissoluble link between verse 3 and verse 6. Paul thus utilized his own ministry to introduce and illustrate the concept of *charisma* as gifting for service.[4] Paul could write to them these instructions because he had received a specific grace, empowering him to minister to them. They too, individually, had received their own grace: "and since we have gifts [*charismata*] that differ according to the grace given to us." How could Paul have better addressed a community unknown to him than to assert that his authority and ability for writing to them were of the very same nature as the abilities which enabled them to fulfill their particular tasks in the community? They were all empowered for unique service by the gifts of God's grace. What better way to introduce the concept of charismatic ministry, to persons with no knowledge of such a teaching, than to illustrate personally the principle he planned to describe? Simply paraphrased, "I can write to you because God has gifted and empowered me to do so, but that simply illustrates that you too are gifted for service." Thus Paul informed them that he, along with them, had received a *charisma* which differed according to the individualized grace entrusted to him.

Notice that the introduction of *charisma* to the Roman community follows the same pattern as that used in the first introduction of the term in 1 Corinthians 1:4-7. In each case the specialized sense of *charisma* was explained by its relationship to *charis*.[5] However in the present context the point is even clearer than in 1 Corinthians because Paul followed it with several illustrations of grace gifts. We must bear in mind that Paul was both introducing the word and the concept of ministry by gifts. They did not attach any special value to this word.

Thus Paul gave it value by the context itself and by the example of his own apostolic gift.

It should be noted that Paul addressed *all believers* with the assurance that *each* believer had been given some potential for service. Paul therefore instructed them to evaluate themselves soberly. The linking with verse 2 is important. The believer, who was being transformed by the renewal of the mind, was now capable of evaluating himself properly. The dual concept—ability to *discern* and potential to *employ* —in the verb *prove* (*dokimazō*) was here applied to the *charismata*. The believer can discern his own charismatic potential (12:3) and can rightly employ his gift (12:6). Thus Paul's emphasis on the renewed mind and consequent sober evaluation served much the same purpose as his discussion of spiritual discernment in 1 Corinthians 2:10-16. In that passage Paul's major emphasis was that the Christian was given discernment so that he might know the things which God had freely given him. Notice that the centrality of *charis* in the discussion of "gifts for service" is even more apparent in Romans than in 1 Corinthians because of the conspicuous absence of any mention of the Spirit in this passage. This again suggests that they were not dealing with the same controversy of gifts as a sign of spirituality as were the Corinthians.

To Each a Measure of Faith

The play on words, "think more highly [*huperphronein*] . . . think [*phronein*] . . . think [*phronein*] . . . sound judgement [*sōphronein*]" gave impact to Paul's insistence on proper evaluation. The first injunction was expressed negatively. Christians must not think more highly of themselves then they ought to think. While it is possible that Paul was combatting a spiritual arrogance which he knew to be present in Rome, it is more likely that "think more highly" was given only in antithesis to "sound judgment." The context shows that Paul's emphasis was on sound judgment and that he was equally concerned with those who might undervalue themselves and thus deprive the body. Paul's strong emphasis on "each" and "all" and his use of the body imagery countered both forms of erroneous thinking. It is quite probable that the danger of overevaluation is explicitly mentioned owning to the recent Corinthian difficulties from which Paul became too painfully aware that spiritual arrogance was an ever-present danger that could disrupt a community in which every member was gifted for ministry.

The problem of overevaluation and underevaluation are still with us and both are equally destructive to the work of the church. Everyone has served on the committee with the individual who can do it all. Implicitly or sometimes explicitly he makes it clear that if everyone else will get out of the way, he can get this project done. This sort of overevaluation ignores the gifts of others and destroys the unity of the body. Perhaps more subtle, but equally devastating to the life of the body is underevaluation. This is the person who simply argues, "I can do nothing. I don't have any gifts or abilities." Often they end their little speech with a pious refrain, "I'll just pray for the rest of you." That sounds pious, but it is not biblical. All members are gifted and this "humble" underevaluation, while often less obnoxious than overevaluation, hurts the body in equal manner.

One's sober evaluation is to be made on the basis that God has distributed to each a measure of faith. The difficult phrase "measure of faith" has elicited a number of tentative solutions, and each in turn has been found to be inadequate by the next commentator. C. E. B. Cranfield's list of eight solutions demonstrates the variety of possibilities.[6] We must therefore pay attention not only to the meaning of the individual words but also to their function as a unit in the present context. There are several truths which the context makes clear. The emphatic "each" makes it clear that "measure of faith" is something which has been "distributed" (KJV) or "apportioned" to every believer. Since the "measure" is something distributed to each, it is likely that it should be translated "portion" or "measured part" (2 Cor. 10:13). Notice however that the emphasis is on the individuality of the portion and not on the quantity. When one soberly evaluates himself with the awareness that he has been given a measure of faith, he discovers his appropriate place in the body where every believer has a function to perform. Finally our interpretation of this phrase must give meaning to the equally difficult and similar phrase "according to the proportion of his faith" in verse 6.

Largely on the basis of the contextual application, a majority of commentators have suggested that the entire phrase is virtually equivalent to saying that each has a *charisma.* The context shows that this suggestion clearly moves in the right direction, but if "measure of faith" is synonymous with *charisma* why did Paul not simply use *charisma?* To understand "measure of faith" properly we must give due consideration to the relationship between the possession of *charisma* and the renewal of the mind which enabled the believer to prove (know and do) the will of God. Paul now specifically applied the two aspects of *proving* to the *discernment* and *utilization* of gifts.

Notice first in verse 3 Paul used sober evaluation with the phrase "measure of faith" to discuss proper *discernment* of one's particular gift. In verse 6 he employed "according to his proportion of faith" and the understood verb "let each exercise them accordingly" to discuss the *utilization* of gifts. The Christian is to evaluate himself soberly, aware that God has given him a specific charismatic potential. But this is more than simply knowing one has a *charisma;* it includes the proper understanding of the nature, goal, and boundaries of one's gift. It is an expression of God's grace, given to edify the body and therefore one should not overly evaluate himself and become arrogant, nor underevaluate himself and become useless.

When *charismata* are rightly discerned, that is to say the nature, goal, and boundaries are recognized, control is inherent within the gifts themselves. External control may of necessity be employed when gifts are abused arrogantly as in Corinth, but that was not an issue in Rome. Each individual can understand that he has been graciously empowered to fulfill a particular function within the community, and therefore he must fully utilize his own gift and appreciate the ministry of those gifted differently (vv. 4-5). This very point is made explicit in verses 6-8 where Paul discussed utilization of charismatic gifts "according to the . . . proportion of faith."

Paul insisted that each person must serve in proportion to his charismatic potential. Notice that faith is not to be taken here in a normal sense of belief in God. Someone *could* then say "I can exercise the gift of prophecy and you only have the gift of giving because I have more faith than you." This could lead to spiritual arrogance which is contrary to the very nature of gifts. Or perhaps they might be tempted to claim that their prophetic gift was more powerful than someone else's gift of prophecy because of their greater faith. In both verse 3 and verse 6 "measure of faith" and "proportion of faith" must be understood by the context. The entire process can be explained thus: having soberly evaluated himself, the prophet is aware of his charismatic potential: his gift, its nature, purpose, and limitations. He now must fully employ his gift with the awareness that his ministry is a gift of grace, with the desire to serve the good of the whole and with the realization that he is only one member of a functioning body.

This principle is expressed in shorthand fashion for the next three gifts (service, teaching, and exhortation) by immediately following each gift with a qualifying phrase appropriate to that gift. For example, one who discerns that he has the gift of service must fully utilize that gift in serving. The phrase "in his serving" was intended to carry forward the three implications mentioned above (nature, purpose, and limitations). In the case of the final three gifts (giving, leading, and showing mercy) the formulation was altered, and they were set in relation to the motives and attitudes which must accompany them. It is not entirely clear why Paul altered the formula at this point. Perhaps it was only for stylistic purposes. Could it be, however, that since the last three gifts described general functions closely related to services of compassion, Paul felt that "according to the proportion" of faith in regard to them was better expressed in terms of accompanying attitudes? For example, the person with the gift of showing mercy would be exercising that gift "according to the measure of faith" when it was accompanied with "cheerfulness." Else it could easily degenerate into a false demonstration of concern. We have all confronted the person who will give people food or clothing, but with an attitude that makes the recipient feel awkward. The person with the gift of mercy will share out of such cheerfulness that the genuineness of the gift will be clear and the recipient will be edified, not demeaned.

The Body Imagery

Verses 4-5 continue the thought of verse 3 by illustrating the necessity and purpose of sober evaluation in the context of the Christian community. In verse 4 Paul presented the illustration from the human body and in verse 5 he applied it to the Christian community. The illustration is straightforward. The human body is a *unit* precisely because it is made up of numerous members, each with a unique function. Each member of the body has a specific role, and therefore each member is equally necessary. No one member can fail to function, nor can any member, no matter how central, fulfill all the functions of the body. The human body provides a particularly appropriate illustration for the gifted community because it clearly illustrates the unique principle that unity is dependent upon diversity and the members are *interdependent.*

Individually gifted members form a functioning body in Christ. In verse 5 Paul broke the parallelism with verse 4 by the addition of the phrase "individually members of one another" (see the thought of 12:10). The personal relationship which existed between members of the community was spelled out in more detail in 1 Corinthians 12:26, but was clearly alluded to here by the phrase "individually members of one another." Since members are integrally linked to one another, they should utilize their gifts for the good of the whole. This Christian unity is such that it does full justice to individuality, and yet emphasizes the good of the whole. Commentators frequently fail to point out one facet of the body imagery that I find particularly important. A proper understanding of gifts causes me to realize how dependent I am on other body members. I cannot function alone in the realm of the spiritual. I not only need the fellowship of the church for my spiritual encouragement, but I need the gifts of the entire body if I am going to be effective in my ministry. This does not just hold true for pastors. It is equally true for every believer.

The Gift List

The gift list of Romans deserves some attention from a broader perspective. While the order of the list may have had some significance, it was not a ranking of value. The primary purpose of this list was to illustrate from a functional perspective the principle introduced to the Roman Christians by Paul in verse 3. It was the demonstration of the truth that all members have some gift for service but that all do not have the same function. The originality and dynamic impact of the Pauline concept of gifted ministry must not be overlooked simply because of our own familiarity through countless readings of Paul's letters. This, no doubt, was for the Romans a new and dramatic expression of the inner workings of the Christian community. Try to hear these truths with the Romans, as it were for the first time. The community is like a functioning body in Christ! Each member is responsible for the welfare of the whole and each one of you is divinely empowered to fulfill a specialized task. You must therefore use your unique grace gifts according to their nature, purpose, and limitation.

The list is broad in perspective although the gifts are few in number. I offered a suggestion as to the specific purpose and content of the two gifts lists in 1 Corinthians, but is that possible in this instance? Several commentators have drawn attention to the absence of enthusiastic or miraculous gifts. The absence of such gifts from the list does not necessarily demonstrate their nonexistence in Rome. Paul may not have had such specific information. However, and more importantly, their absence tells us something about Paul's emphasis. The gifts in this list fall into two major categories: leadership gifts and service gifts.

Prophecy and teaching were encountered in 1 Corinthians 12:28. Service (*diakonia*), because of its location between prophecy and teaching, merits a translation more specific than "service." It may be that *diakonia* here pointed to a "regularized" ministry existing in some, if not all, early congregations and is thus comparable to the usage in Philippians 1:1. Thus we find that our deacons (same Greek word) are gifted by God to serve the congregation. One must ask whether we look for deacons today who have the gift of service. Do we simply look for those who are well known in the church or deserve the honor?

The ministry indicated by exhortation was commended to all in 1 Thessalonians 5:12, discussed as a part of the prophet's task in 1 Corinthians 14:3, and regularly practiced by the apostle Paul. Its location in this list and its formulation "he who exhorts in his exhortation" which is like that of the preceding gifts, may suggest a specific leadership function. We simply do not have sufficient evidence to be certain. Its presence warns against the attempt to construct a well-defined official hierarchy from the first four gifts and against dividing the list too artificially.

The final three gifts are discussed with some difficulty by many commentators because they do not fit their narrow definition of *charisma.* Yet they are some of the most unique and exciting gifts in any listing of gifts. "He who gives with liberality" no doubt referred to the compassionate sharing of one's own possessions for the benefit of others (see 1 Cor. 13:3, 2 Cor. 8:3-7). I have often said in jest that I have never heard too many folks claiming this gift. On one occasion when I was preaching on this section I had a young wife who came to me with a huge smile on her face. She exclaimed that for the first time she really understood her husband. She remarked that he loved to give. She said giving made him come alive and gave purpose to his labor. All of us are called to be good stewards in our giving, but there are some who have a unique gift for giving with great liberality. Perhaps we would find others who would claim this special gift if we taught that it was available.

"He who shows mercy with cheerfulness" probably had in mind functions such as tending the sick, relieving the poor, or caring for the aged and disabled. Notice that these benevolent tasks must be accompanied with cheerfulness. When this is truly one's gift it never becomes a duty and thus does not exhibit a sense of drudgery. "He who leads" can be translated "the one leading or presiding" (see 1 Thess. 5:12; 1 Tim. 3:4 *ff.*, 5:17) or "the one giving aid." Its location between "he who gives" and "he who shows mercy" may recommend the latter translation. Thus the final three gifts describe comprehensive ministries for service. This list makes it clear that all abilities for service to the body when soberly evaluated and rightly employed will be seen as *charismata*.

We must draw attention to an interesting comparison with the gift list in 1 Corinthians 12:28. There Paul was arguing against the narrow perspective of the *pneumatika* (miraculous gifts) held by the spirituals. He "stretched" the gift list to demonstrate that the leaders were empowered by God for their tasks and that "mundane" abilities for service were *charismata*. The only two areas of gifts mentioned in Romans 12 correspond with the two areas stressed by their inclusion in 1 Corinthians 12:28. In 1 Corinthians 12 and 14, Paul demonstrated his preference for the more edifying and less dramatic gifts. I suggest that the gifts listed here in Romans 12:6-8 give us no information about the community in Rome but rather give us an insight into Paul's passion to stress the gifts of leadership/proclamation and service.

The freedom with which Paul referred to *persons* and *gifts* is quite clearly evidenced in the movement in this list from abstract to concrete. In 1 Corinthians 12:28 Paul began with persons (apostles, prophets) and moved to abilities (miracles, gifts of healing). Here he began with abilities and moved to persons. What is interesting here is the flexibility with which Paul could move from concrete to abstract and personal to impersonal. Paul could speak of prophets in one listing of gifts (1 Cor. 12:28) and about prophecy in another (Rom. 12:6). Now it is clear that the person was not the gift, but the relationship between the individual and the gift possessed was so integral that an individual could be referred to in terms of the gift. The teacher could be called "he who teaches" because he possessed the gift of teaching. It is clear that one's gift is effective and identifiable only in the act of ministry, but there is never an indication that one's gift departs when he is not functioning. I cannot agree with those who see spiritual gifts as momentary empowering for service.

It is interesting that the first few gifts are practically synonymous with "official" leadership functions, whereas the second half of the list includes gifts representative of very general ministries of service. The impact is similar to that if 1 Corinthians 12:28, but without poiemical overtones. There exist side by side in the charismatic community "leaders" who are empowered for service by God and "members" who have their own unique service roles. Paul apparently saw no conflict between these two principles.

Before concluding, it is appropriate to reiterate the point made earlier about the location of this gift passage. Immediately following the gift list is a series of ethical demands. While the particular instructions may reflect traditional Christian teaching, their intent in the present context is of some importance. We noted previously that the gift passage is surrounded by ethical teaching, and now we should also notice that the content of this section is similar to that of 1 Corinthians 13 (See table at the end of this chapter.) Verse 9 serves as the bridge between the two sections, and thus "Let love be without hyprocrisy" becomes a heading for all that follows. Both sections are addressed to all believers.

Why did Paul literally surround his teaching on gifts with ethical instruction? Several suggestions might be made: (1) The lack of ethical concern was such a prominent part of the Corinthian aberration, that even here Paul wanted to discuss gifts in the context of ethical behavior. (2) *Charisma* and love both have their origin in God and are indicative of the believer's relationship with God. "Living sacrifice" (KJV) expresses total obedience, and this is the necessary prerequisite both for proper utilization of gifts and for ethical living. (3) In like manner, the renewed mind enables the believer to prove the will of God, "That which is good and acceptable and perfect" (v. 2), and to evaluate himself soberly and thus to discover and embrace his charismatic potential. (4) *Charisma* and love occur together because together they embrace all Christian existence. Love has the broader context encompassing Christian existence in the context of the worshiping community and in the broader community. On the other hand *charismata* are primarily related to edification of the body. The spiritual person will express love by means of *charisma,* but this is not the only channel for the visible expression of love. Thus by thrusting the discussion of *charisma* into the forefront of the teaching section (chs. 12—15), Paul illustrated both the potential and limitations of *charisma.*

Conclusions

(1) The general tenor of Romans and especially 12:3-8 demonstrates that this passage functioned as a brief and non-polemical presentation of general principles for the functioning community and did not therefore reflect a specific situation in Rome.

(2) Paul placed the discussion of gifts in an ethical teaching context for several interrelated reasons, the most important of which was to put *charisma* into the proper perspective against the backdrop of the whole of Christian existence.

(3) In a fashion similar to 1 Corinthians, Paul emphasized that every believer was charismatically endowed, that unity emerges from diversity and that members of the body are interdependent. These points were made in summary fashion owing to the nature of the passage.

(4) The ability of the spiritual person to understand properly the things given by God (see 1 Cor. 2:12) was made explicit with the concept of the renewal of the mind and specifically applied to gifts with the phrase "measure of faith." With this phrase, Paul applied the concept of discernment to the proper evaluation of one's charismatic potential—the understanding of the nature, intent, and limitations of one's ability for service. The similar "according to the proportion of his faith" denoted the practical application of the insight gained through the discerning process described in verse 3. This phrase governs the entire list. As each must evaluate himself according to "measure of faith," so each must employ his gift "according to the proportion of his faith." This does not mean that one person's gifts are more vital than another's because he exercises more faith.

(5) In contrast to 1 Corinthians 14, no rules were given for controlling the gifts. The only "controls" or "limitations" given here were those inherent in the gifts when rightly discerned and utilized.

(6) The prominent use of grace (*charis*) and grace gift (*charismata*)

stressed the given nature and divine source of all abilities for service. There was no mention of the *Spirit* in relation to the gifts. This absence may reflect Paul's recent controversy with the spirituals in Corinth. Paul chose to underline the fact that God was the ultimate source of all *charismata*.

(7) Grace (*charis*) in Romans 12:3 and 6 refers to the particularization of grace in the empowering for ministry. *Charis* comes to focus in the individual as *charisma*—the ability enabling one to function creatively in the body. Although *charisma* becomes visible in activity, it is not to be identified with activity or function. It is not lost when not in use.

(8) The listing of gifts is brief but comprehensive because it was intended to demonstrate a teaching which would have been new to the Romans. The gifts fall into two broad areas: gifts of leadership and gifts of service. This, I think, gives us a fair indication of those gifts which Paul would emphasize in a neutral situation (see the discussion of 1 Cor. 12:28).

(9) The suggestion that for Paul a leader is recognized only because of his *charisma* is not really to the point. All possess *charisma*, but some have leadership functions. With the term *charisma* Paul told us nothing about authority, but only about the nature and source of an ability for ministry. Paul recognized, along with his concept of every-member ministry, a God-given structure in which some must be recognized as leaders (1 Thess. 5:12; 1 Cor. 12:28, 16:16). These concepts are not contradictory nor identical but parallel.

Notes

1. "The Concept of Faith in Paul's Letters to the Romans," *Biblical Research* 13 (1968), 41-53, 42-46 and "*Die Empfänger des Römerbriefes*," *Studia Theologica* 25 (1971), 81-89.

2. Paul S. Minear, *The Obedience of Faith.* (London: SCM, 1971.)

3. J. Chrysostum, *Homilies* XXIX, (1).

4. The term *charisma* occurs five times in Romans prior to its use here (1:11, 5:15-16 [twice], 6:23 and 11:29). In every case the meaning must be determined from the context and not by any special meaning inherent in the word itself.

5. I suggest that the following possible relationship between *charis* and *charisma.* The *charisma* is the visible expression in the individual of the specialized *charis* given to him. For example: a specific empowering for service is received (*charis*), and it is manifested in the individual as the potential or ability to serve (*charisma* = *diakonia*) which then must be utilized in service (Romans 12:6), or again, although somewhat differently expressed: an empowering for teaching is received (*charis*). It is so integrally related to the person that he can be called "teacher" or one who has the *charisma* of teaching. He must then employ this gift "in the teaching."

6. C. E. B. Cranfield, "METRON ΠΙΣΤΕΩΣ in Romans 12:3," *New Testament Studies* 8 (1961-62), 345-351.

TABLE : PARALLELS OF THOUGHT (NASB)

I Cor. 13		Rom. 12:9-21	
4	Love is patient,	18	If possible, so far as it depends on you, be at peace with all men.
	Love is kind,	13	contributing to the needs of the saints, practicing hospitality (see v. 20).
	and is not jealous;	16a	Be of the same mind toward one another;
	love does not brag	16b	do not be haughty in mind, but associate with the lowly
	and is not arrogant,	16c	Do not be wise in your own estimation.
5	does not act unbecomingly;	17b	Respect what is right in the sight of all men.
	it does not seek its own,	10	Be devoted to one another in brotherly love; give preference to one another in honor;
	is not provoked,	17a	Never pay back evil for evil to anyone.
		19a	Never take your own revenge (see v. 18),
	does not take into account a wrong suffered,	14	Bless those who curse you; bless and curse not.
6	does not rejoice in unrighteousness,	9a	Abhor what is evil;
	but rejoices with the truth	9b	Cling to what is good.
7	bears all things,	15	Rejoice with those who rejoice, and weep with those who weep.
	believes all things,		
	hopes all things,	12a	rejoicing in hope,
	endures all things.	12b	persevering in tribulation,
8	love never fails;	21b	overcome evil with good.

7
Gifted Leaders Equipping Gifted Members

The Hemphills enjoy family vacations. We're not really tourists in the classical sense of that word when it comes to vacation time. We just enjoy getting away and spending the time together as a family. We have one tradition that has become an informal part of all of our vacations. We work a large jigsaw puzzle as a family project. We are not really jigsaw puzzle fans. In fact, we work only one or two a year and those on our vacation. Each year as our children have gotten older the puzzles have become increasingly complex. This past year was no exception. The puzzle was the picture of numerous baskets of strawberries. You can't possibly believe how many subtle shades of red there are in hundreds of strawberries.

At first the task seemed impossible. There were so many pieces, all of them were so small, and with five of us working at once there was little agreement on how we should even start. I recommended the border, another family member wanted to do a large and prominent basket right in the middle of the picture. Progress was slow during the first few sessions of our puzzle working. Slowly but surely an outline began to emerge, details began to take shape and then true excitement was felt by all as the picture began to take shape. Toward the end all that remained were a few areas of detail that needed to be completed with the missing pieces.

Our study together has perhaps some resemblance to our family's puzzle project. The topic of spiritual gifts is at first so confusing and potentially volatile that we are afraid to begin. Once the courage to start has been mustered, we must then decide on a strategy for study.

152

We've certainly accomplished these two steps. By reading thus far you have shown your desire to learn and the courage to begin. We have consistently followed a strategy of taking the passages in their chronological order while paying careful and strict attention to the historical setting. Many of you will have recognized this is not the only way to work on this topic, but it is one which has been helpful for many. Hopefully, by this time you have developed a clearer picture of Paul's teaching on this matter. It is my greatest hope that for many readers there remain only a few points of detail that need clarification. For example: "How do gifted leaders and gifted members work together for the good of the fellowship?"

The Ephesian letter will provide our last major passage. It contains a verse that is frequently quoted by pastors and laypersons alike about the inner working of the church. "He gave some . . . as pastors and teachers for the equipping of the saints for the work of service, to the building up of the body of Christ (Eph. 4:11)." But what does that mean in the present context? How does it work? How does it fit into the picture of the gifted community as boldly painted in 1 Corinthians 12—14 or Romans 12? These are a few of the detail areas that we hope to clarify as we study Ephesians 4:1-16.

The Ephesian Difficulties

Ephesians is certainly one of the most loved of all the letters in the New Testament. It contains beautiful passages about the believers' inheritance in Christ, their boldness, and their confident access to the Father. The beautiful word picture, which compares the believers' relationship to Christ with that of marital commitment, is in the fifth chapter. Believers of every generation have been given comfort and strength by the powerful description of the whole armor of God.

Nonetheless, the careful reader will notice that the tone and style of this letter is different from that of many of the other Pauline Letters. This very fact, along with other considerations such as vocabulary, doctrine, and history have led some scholars to argue that this letter was written by someone other than Paul. However, when all the evidence concerning these matters is examined there is nothing conclusive that would dictate against accepting the statement of authorship in the first verse: "Paul an apostle of Christ Jesus."

Yet we cannot simply ignore certain facts pointed out by scholars who have argued against Pauline authorship. Why is there a lack of personal rememberances in a letter addressed to a community that was very dear to Paul? One of the scenes that has been etched in my mind from the Book of Acts is of the elders from Ephesus as they embraced Paul before he set sail from Miletus. Paul was intent on reaching Jerusalem before Pentecost. After discussing his situation with these beloved leaders, all were aware that this would perhaps be their last meeting face to face. What a picture of intimacy we find. "And when he said these things, he knelt down and prayed with them all. And they began to weep loud and embraced Paul, and repeatedly kissed him, grieving especially over the word which he had spoken, that they should see his face no more" (Acts 20:36-38a). Is it not reasonable to suspect that Paul would have greeted these beloved leaders or their beloved church in a more personal way?

We must confess also that the tone and style of the letter are different from other more personal letters. The language is often the language of prayer. It is also obvious to the careful reader that the content and even the phrasing of Colossians and Ephesians are very similar. How do we account for these unique features of Ephesians?

If we can assert that arguments about language, style, and doctrine do not rule against Pauline authorship, we are required to establish a setting within the lifetime of Paul which makes sense of the content of this letter. Thus we must return to the essential questions of history that we have asked in relation to each passage we have dealt with. What is the setting and purpose of the letter?

A Letter to Combat Heresy in Asia Minor

The general tone of the letter and the lack of personal rememberances make it unlikely that the Ephesian Letter was addressed to a particular congregation, especially one known to Paul. Notice, for example, that in 1:15-16 Paul assured them that he had not ceased praying for them since he had heard of the faith that existed among them. In chapter 3:1-2 Paul introduced himself by including a special reference to his ministry to the Gentiles. Such a reference would hardly be necessary in a church where Paul had ministered for at least two years (Acts 19:1-20).

Many scholars who argue for Pauline authorship have suggested that Ephesians was a circular letter, one intended for more than one church. Yet they often follow that conclusion with the suggestion that is so general in nature as to be nothing more than a last will and testament of Paul. The close linking of the content of Ephesians and Colossians and the specific nature of the content of the letter argue against the idea that Ephesians is nothing more than a summation of Pauline teaching. Can we then suggest a purpose for Paul's writing a circular letter and describe a historical situation which illuminated the letter and at the same time takes into consideration its general nature, unusual style, language, and emphasis?

We know that while Paul was in prison he came into contact with Epaphras (Col. 4:12; Philemon 1:23). Epaphras was apparently a leader or the pastor in the church at Colossae (Col. 1:7-8). It appears that he shared with Paul information concerning heretical teachings which were creating difficulties for the church at Colossae and requested his assistance. Therefore Paul wrote Colossians at the request of Epaphras. In that letter he dealt with the difficulties at Colossae in a straightforward and specific manner.

No doubt, the news that heretical teachings were affecting this neighboring congregation caused Paul to fear for the church of Ephesus and other churches throughout proconsular Asia. In Acts 19:10 we are told that Paul's ministry in Ephesus had a profound effect on all who lived in Asia. It is not improbable that many of the churches like those in Colossae and Laodicea owed their origin to Paul's work in Ephesus. Perhaps Epaphras was converted and discipled by Paul in Ephesus and then returned to Colossae to begin that church. Thus having written this specific letter to the church at Colossae, Paul seized the opportunity to write a more general and positive letter with the specific intention of stopping the spread of similar heretical teachings throughout Asia.

By this reconstruction Paul had written two letters which must be delivered by hand. Colossians was specific and was addressed to a particular community. Ephesians was more general and was intended for several churches in Asia. Paul was prepared to dispatch Tychicus, a beloved brother and faithful servant with these two letters (Col. 4:7), but one complicating factor still remained. Another visitor to Paul while he was in prison was Onesimus, a runaway slave. Onesimus had apparently been converted under Paul's ministry and thus was now a "beloved brother" (Col. 4:9). Yet Paul had to return him to his owner Philemon, "a beloved brother and fellow worker" (Philem. 1:1) in the church of Colossae. Paul desired that Onesimus be freed and treated as a brother, but felt an obligation to allow his owner, Philemon, to make the decision.

Tychicus was dispatched, accompanied by the runaway slave Onesimus, bearing three letters: Ephesians, Colossians, and Philemon. Tychicus traveled by sea, landing at Ephesus. Here he delivered the letter we know as Ephesians with the instructions that it should be shared with other churches of proconsular Asia. It would have been natural for a letter from Paul intended to strengthen the churches in Asia Minor to originate from Ephesus since this was a central seaport location which had been the focal point of Paul's ministry in Asia. This may also account for the fact that some early manuscripts of the Ephesian letter do not contain the words "at Ephesus" in verse 1. Could this letter have been originally circulated with no specific community name? The words "at Ephesus" may have later been added because of its strong connections with Ephesus, its city of origin. Perhaps it originally had a blank in the introduction so that each new copy could be personalized for the recipient church.

We can make one further tentative suggestion concerning the actual destination of this letter. I think it was originally intended for the seven churches mentioned in the book of Revelation: Ephesus, Smyrna, Pergamum, Thyatira, Sardis, Philadelphia, and Laodicea. William Ramsey, a great scholar from a generation passed, suggested that these seven churches made up a Christian mail route.[1] They were in a sense an early association of like-minded churches who cultivated fellowship and friendship through a vital communication link. After delivering our Ephesian Letter to Ephesus, Tychicus, because he feared for the safety of Onesimus, proceeded with Onesimus and the letters to Colossae and Philemon directly to Colossae by way of the Meander Valley. If you check your map in the back of your Bible you will be able to trace out the separate routes of "Ephesians" and of Tychicus. You will notice that Tychicus took the route by the Meander Valley which was more direct and less populated. This would provide a safer route for conveying a runaway slave.

There are several verses in these two letters that make this reconstruction even more appealing. According to Colossians 4:15-16, Paul wanted the Colossians to share their letter with the Laodiceans and to read the letter from Laodicea. Laodicea would have been the final stop on the route suggested above. The letter from Laodicea then is the letter we now call Ephesians. The content of Ephesians would have been particularly valuable to the Colossians because it was written by Paul to address the very problems they were facing.

Notice further in the Colossian letter that Paul indicated his concern was not only for those in Colossae and Laodicea, but also "for all those who have not personally seen my face" (2:1). Could it be that Paul wanted the Colossian Letter itself to be shared with a larger audience. The churches which received Ephesians were promised a personal visit by Tychicus (Eph. 6:21-22; see Col. 4:7-8). Tychicus, after his present mission, could visit each of the churches, carrying with him a copy of the Colossian Letter, and explain the full purpose behind these unexpected Pauline epistles.

There is one other small verse that is made meaningful by this suggestion. In Ephesians 3:3-4, we read: ". . . as I wrote to you in brief, and by referring to this, when you read you can understand my insight into the mystery of Christ." The tenses of the verbs (aorist followed by a present participle) suggest that Paul was referring to something that was already written. When this previously written document was available for reading, it would explain more fully Paul's authority for writing and the reason behind this present letter. This verse has long been a puzzle, and therefore some have suggested that the verse refers to all of the Pauline letters in a collection or simply to the previous chapters of Ephesians. I think that the Colossian Letter best suits this description and fulfills this function. The specific arguments in Colossians would further explain Paul's concern for the churches of proconsular Asia.

I suggest therefore that not only was the Ephesian Letter circulated among the seven churches, but that Tychicus personally visited these churches with a copy of the Colossian Letter traveling on a reverse route from Laodicea to Ephesus. Many of these suggestions must remain in the realm of speculation since there is no way to verify them. Nevertheless, the historical and theological relationship of the two letters does not depend on the believability of my reconstruction of the distribution of these two letters. The single most important point is that the two letters were written in response to the same heretical problems and therefore contain complimentary messages.

Identifying the Colossian Heresy

Since I have suggested that the Colossian heresy prompted Paul to write Ephesians, it would be helpful to briefly understand the problems in Colossae. The description of the Colossian heresy is complex and a full investigation is unnecessary for this present work. The problems addressed are so diverse that it seems unlikely that there was a group of opponents in Colossae with a theological agenda. It appears that here we encounter a community which was under pressure to conform to the beliefs and practices of its pagan and Jewish neighbors. For our purposes, it will be sufficient to note briefly some of the symptoms of the problem.

The evidence from Colossians suggests that there were some individuals who claimed to possess a deep wisdom and insight into God's will (Col. 1:9-14; 2:2-4,8). These claims may have been based on visionary experiences (2:18). There was a tendency by some not to give Christ the exalted place which was accorded to Him by the Christian community (Col. 1:15-20; 2:8-10). Not only were the influences of pagan immorality present but there were those who practiced self-denial (2:16-25). Their decrees were: "Do not handle, do not taste, do not touch!" (Col. 2:21). All of these factors presented a challenge to the validity and historical continuity of the church. Was the church nothing more than another religious sect? Was Jesus the unique Son of God who reveals the Father?

Companion Letters

Several unique features of Ephesians are made meaningful if we treat Ephesians and Colossians as companion letters to counter the confusion of the various heresies being heard in Asia Minor. First, Paul faced a communication problem since his letters would be read by several communities which he had not personally founded. Notice that Ephesians 3:1 contains an explicit identification of the writer which might otherwise appear unnecessary and artificial. Why would Paul need to establish his authority if he was personally known to all the recipients? References to Paul's imprisonment are common in the epistles written from prison, but in Ephesians the mention of imprisonment was specifically related to his Gentile mission. The phrase "the prisoner of Christ Jesus" is further qualified by the phrase "for the sake of you Gentiles" (3:1). Paul could write to these predominately Gentile congregations because he was a prisoner on their behalf. Paul also mentioned his special gift of grace to minister to the Gentiles twice in his letter (3:2, 7-8). Paul's message was authoritative since it was based on his insight into the mystery of Christ concerning God's plan for a body made up of Jews and Gentiles alike.

Following his discussion of the reconcilation of Jew and Gentile alike in one body, Paul described the church as having been built on the foundation of the *holy* apostles and prophets. The phrase is striking and was intended to grant assurance to the struggling Gentile communities by underlining the historical continuity of the church and the divine authority of Paul's message. Only God's *holy* apostles and prophets have recognized and proclaimed God's plan concerning the true nature of the church made up of Jew and Gentile alike. The parallel passage in Colossians 1:24-29 served the same purpose and has much the same content as this section. In Colossians (1:25-26) Paul bluntly declared that the message he had shared came from God.

They need not seek another means for deeper insight into God's will since Christ is the wisdom of God (2:2-3) and Paul had preached Christ.

Second, Paul's concern to communicate effectively his genuine pastoral concern may fully account for the language of prayer and praise. How could the apostle more effectively communicate his concern, for these folks unknown to him face to face, than by sharing the actual content of his prayers on their behalf. This is not to say that the language of prayer in Ephesians is nothing more than an emotional device used to communicate a message thinly disguised as prayer. Most of us have witnessed the individuals who use prayer to get their message across in a Sunday School class or business meeting—like the man who prayed: "Lord we want Your will on this matter and so I pray that You would help these folks to see clearly what I am proposing." That is using manipulation veiled as prayer—not at all Paul's intent.

Here we catch a very real glimpse into the powerful prayer life of the apostle Paul. Since Epaphras had informed Paul concerning the heretical influences threatening the churches of proconsular Asia, Paul had not ceased to pray for them (Col. 2:1; Eph. 1:15-16). It is understandable therefore that there was an almost unconscious vaciliation between prayer and teaching in the first three chapters. As mentioned before, some scholars have objected to Pauline authorship based on the language and style of Ephesians. I believe that the language and style are to be explained primarily in terms of Paul's actual prayers on behalf of these communities. Thus we are given the unique privilege of almost listening in on the impassioned prayers of a concerned apostle.

Third, the authority and dominion of Christ over all the universe was the prominent theme used by Paul to combat the Colossian heresy (Col. 1:13-23, 2:8-9). In Ephesians, Paul took this same theme and used it positively to affirm these threatened communities by demonstrating the ongoing relationship of Christ, who is Lord over all things, to the church (see especially Eph. 1:20-23). Paul normally used the word *church (ekklēsia)* in his earlier writings to refer to a specific local congregation. While the concept of the broader body of Christ is sometimes found in the earlier letters, it is striking that *church* in Ephesians refers only to the broader church. The emphasis on the universal church, made up of all true believers everywhere, was no doubt related to the fact that Paul was addressing several different communities. Furthermore he wanted them to be aware of the larger church so they might be mutually benefitted by establishing relationships one with another. Yet, the major purpose of this bold use of the term *church* was to give positive assurance to these communities who were being treated as simply another cult or having their validity questioned because they were predominantly Gentile. They were indeed "The Church," the very body of Christ.

Paul thus underlined the historical authority of the church by indicating that it was built upon the foundation of the apostles (New Testament witness) and the prophets (Old Testament writers) with Christ Himself as the cornerstone (Eph. 2:20). This mystery had been revealed to the holy apostles and prophets (3:4-6). Paul declared that Jew and Gentile alike had received the riches of God's grace (2:4-16). Those who were once far off had now been brought near in the blood of Christ and He has made of two, one new body (2:13-18). Paul thus assured these predominantly Gentile congregations that they were fellow heirs, fellow members of the body, and fellow partakers of the promise. This church, composed of Jew and Gentile alike, is the fulness of Christ, who is the Head over all things (Eph. 1:20-23; see 3:16-21; 4:10-16). This emphasis on the dominion of Christ in Colossians and the application of this truth to the *church* in Ephesians can be seen as complementary: the former dealing with the Colossian heresy explicitly, the latter a positive effort to prevent its spread. Let's not ignore this beautiful and exalting message on the church. We are sometimes guilty of treating the church as just another institution or organization. Thus we play church by going through the motions of church activities without fully recognizing or utilizing the resources made available through the ressurected Christ for the empowering of His church.

In the light of the many similarities between Colossians and Ephesians, the differences take on special significance. It is noteworthy, therefore, that a passage concerning gifts for ministry is a prominent feature of Ephesians, but altogether lacking from Colossians. Why did Paul include a gift passage in the Ephesian Letter which was intended for churches he did not know personally? We should note that there is no indication in either of the letters that any of the difficulties being faced by the communities had been created by a misunderstanding of spiritual gifts as was the case with Corinth. The content of Ephesians 4:1-16 does not suggest that Paul sensed any difficulties in this area. What then is the purpose of this section and how do we relate it to Paul's overall treatment of the empowering of the New Testament church?

This last question is one of immense importance since there are Bible scholars who think that this passage is inconsistent with earlier Pauline teaching on gifts. Some have gone so far as to say that the vision of a gifted community has faded. It is true that there are new emphases and insights, but I believe that these locate themselves quite comfortably in the continuation of Paul's thought when these companion letters are interpreted in light of their historical situation.

The Context of Ephesians 4:1-16

The *therefore* indicates that there is an intended link between the discussion that follows and that which preceded. This passage logically flows out of Ephesians 1—3. Paul entreated the readers to live in a manner worthy of their calling. This exhortation was based on the content of the previous chapters: they had been chosen (1:4), called (1:18), and made alive by God's grace (2:5). Notice that the phrase: "worthy of the calling with which you have been called" served a purpose similar to that of "by the mercies of God" in Romans 12:1. In both instances there was a specific reminder of their present standing in Christ. These believers must never forget that they were "sons of disobedience" (2:2), but God who is "rich in mercy" (2:4) had enabled them to enter a grace relationship with Himself (2:5-10) and thus they were made members of God's household. It is a household of faith built upon the foundation of the apostles and prophets, with

Christ Himself as the cornerstone. This is the basis for the call to consistent living and service in the Christian community.

I often wonder whether this awesome sense of history is lacking in our churches today. Sometimes I feel a sense of ingratitude on our part because we tend to forget what our situation would be if it were not for God's great love for us. There are times as a father that I get upset with my children because they grumble and complain about the tasks assigned to them. They want all the privileges and advantages of the household without any responsibility. I find it helpful to remind them of the sacrifices made on their behalf not only by their parents but by other generations. Are we sometimes apathetic in our service to the Lord and our commitment to His body, the church, because we have forgotten what God has done for us in Christ Jesus? You will remember that Paul expressed his sense of calling as a obligation that made him eager to serve (Rom. 1:14-15). Perhaps we need a constant reminder to walk worthy of our calling. Does your service express the gratitude and love of one who was once alienated and afar off who has now been brought near and granted sonship?

This truth forms the basis for the requirements of the next several chapters. It is the foundation for unity, mutual service, the demand for moral integrity, and unity in the home, and so forth. Thus we notice again that the actual discussion of gifts for ministry (4:7-16) is both preceded and followed by ethical instruction and bound to the total life of the church, as was the case in Romans 12:3-8. The theme of the worthy walk is introduced in 4:1 and then specifically taken up again in 4:17 *ff.* with the repetition of the word *walk.* This term occurs again in 5:2,8, and 15, and in each case it pushes forward this central theme. Keep in mind this context as we seek to understand Paul's purpose for discussing gifts for ministry.

The Worthy Walk and Community Relationships

Paul fortified his entreaty with a reference to his status as a prisoner of the Lord. This reference recalled the force of 3:1, where Paul explained the basis for his writing to these congregations which did not know him by personal experience. The reference to imprisonment has a function similar to the phrase "For through the grace given to me" in Romans 12:3, where Paul, in a similar situation, explained his rationale for writing to a community which he had not founded.

The description of the manner of the worthy walk in the life of the community begins in verse 2. The principal idea is expressed by the phrase "showing forbearance to one another in love," which indicates the ability of love to overcome the dangers inherent in human relationships (see 1 Cor. 13:4-7). This verse is not about being virtuous, but about living in harmony with God's call. We could well compare this verse to the nature of Christ or the fruit of the Spirit. These are attributes produced by the Spirit of God in the life of the person who has been saved by grace and has become the workmanship of God (2:8-10). All too often we fall into the trap of trying to produce these virtues. We try to be patient or humble and become frustrated when we are not. These cannot be produced by human striving—they are the divine work of the Spirit and thus they come through surrender.

Little is gained by discussing the actual number of virtues listed here or how the phrases should be linked together. The terms somewhat overlap in meaning and together they were intended to combat arrogance, harshness, and intolerance in personal relationships. These virtues are the necessary backdrop for the proper functioning of a gifted community.

Humility and gentleness can be taken together since they are linked together in the Greek construction. Humility is a distinctly biblical virtue, and was actually considered a vice in the Greek world. Humility is the opposite of complacency, conceit, and self-exaltation. It is not a pious, personal put-down, such as is condemned in Colossians 2:23, but it is a *proper evaluation* of oneself based on the understanding that one totally depends upon the grace of God. Therefore the underlying meaning is virtually the same as the call for sober evaluation in Romans 12:3. The proper evaluation of oneself in the light of God's grace rules out the possibility for arrogance and enables one to be *gentle* in relationships with others.

Humility, gentleness, and patience are the divine attributes, the practical expressions of love which enable believers to forbear with one another in love and thus to preserve the unity of the Spirit (v. 3). It is love in all its practical expressions which must govern the Christian life and specifically the human relationships which take place within the context of the community. This theme is amplified in 4:17-32, where Paul reminded the believers that they must be renewed in the spirit of the mind (see Rom. 12:2), put on the new self (v. 24), and behave accordingly because they are members one of another (vv. 25 *ff.*). It should come as no surprise that we continue to hear both the emphasis and terminology of earlier gift passages.

In any community situation there is the danger of personal confrontation, individual arrogance, and the resulting disunity. These problems often center around capacities for service and leadership positions within the church. In 1 Thessalonians 5:12 *ff.* Paul admonished the brethren to esteem their leaders highly in love, to live in peace, to help the weak, to be patient with all, and to show forbearance when wronged. Paul, faced with the exaggerated claims of the spirituals and their self-centered life-styles, placed the description of the authentic spiritual person at the heart of the discussion of gifts in 1 Corinthians 13. He then proceeded in chapter 14 to demonstrate the practical effects of the outworking of love in the life of the gifted community. The Corinthian aberration made Paul acutely aware of the danger of spiritual arrogance about capacities for service and its effects on the life of the community. Consequently, in Romans 12, he placed the discussion of gifts for service in the context of ethical behavior and underlined the necessity for proper evaluation of one's gifted potential. The proper Christian attitude was so much at the forefront of Paul's mind in the Roman correspondence that three of the gifts were listed with the attitude appropriate to them (Rom. 12:8). Therefore it is not surprising that in Ephesians Paul again surrounded the discussion of the ministering community with the more comprehensive concern of the behavior appropriate to the new life in Christ.

We should not ignore this repeated lesson from Paul. Gifts have meaning only in the context of the community. To be used in an appropriate manner they must be understood as expressions of God's grace. They enable the believer to concretely express love through the edification of the brethren. Yet because no one has all the gifts, they actually make us totally dependent on one another. Therefore the gifts can function properly only when they are exercised with humility, gentleness, patience, and love. If we truly focused on these principles, think how much dissension would be eliminated from the church today.

Unity as Gift and Goal

How could Paul say in one breath that Christians are given unity by the one God and Father, and in the very next breath exhort the readers to preserve the unity? This may at first seem puzzling, but it is precisely the focus of this section, Paul boldly affirmed the unity of believers by denoting seven great unifying truths Christians hold in common. But in equally strong terms he asserted that God has gifted believers for the work of service, to the building up of the body of Christ, "until we all attain to the unity of the faith" (v. 13).

The key thought is still that of "showing forebearance to one another in love." It is mutual forebearance in love that makes possible the exhoration to preserve the unity of the Spirit (v. 3). The unity of the Spirit is unity which is produced by the Holy Spirit through conversion as verse 4 makes plain. The unity of the Spirit points to the experience of grace which all believers share in Christ (see 2:17-18). The theme of unity in the gifted community was first given particular emphasis by Paul in 1 Corinthians 12, where it was stressed by the use of the numeral *one,* which occurred nine times in 1 Corinthians 12 in a way that stressed unity. The body imagery was then introduced to illustrate the practical need for unity. Again you should recall that this unity was based on the common experience of the Spirit which enabled them to confess "Jesus is Lord" (12:3). In Romans 12, unity was given some attention (Rom. 12:5,16, 18), but it again became a *prominent* theme in the Ephesians' gift passage.

Paul elaborated on the divine giveness of unity in a most eloquent way in Ephesians 4:4-6 by presenting the sevenfold unity of the Christian experience. Each of the seven members is emphasized by the repetition of the word *one* with each member. It is difficult to decide whether this sevenfold expression of unity was an original composition for this letter or the use by Paul of a confession of faith used by early Christians at baptism. This is not a crucial issue. The impact would be virtually the same since the readers would, in any case, be reminded of their own baptismal experience.

The first triad—"one body," "one Spirit," "one hope of your calling"—recalls several concepts given full discussion in the first three chapters. "One body" refers to the church as the body of Christ (see 1:23; 2:16; 4:12,16), and Spirit refers to the Holy Spirit who in dwells the church and gives it unity (see 2:18,22; 4:3). The church is a spiritual organism, made up of persons who have the shared experience of the Spirit in common, and thus it derives its life, unity, and ministries from the Spirit who is the gift of the ascended Lord. The phrase "just as also you were called in one hope of your calling" means the hope which is received by virtue of one's response to the call to salvation (1:18 and 2:12). In 1:18 Paul prayed that the readers might know what is the hope of His calling. Christians were once without hope (2:12) but now they have been given purpose and life through their relationship in Christ.

The second triad—"one Lord," "one faith," "one baptism"—probably appealed to the moment when the Christian confessed Jesus as Lord as he descended into the water of baptism. It is certainly possible that this was a reference to the confession made by believers at their actual water baptism, but the deeper significance is that there is only *one baptism*—into Christ. Thus the primary reference is to the relationship one has with Christ which has been established through belief in Him (1:13,15,19; 3:12) and signified through baptism. Their baptism into Christ had broken down all barriers that could divide them (see Gal. 3:26-28). Remember that this truth was also emphasized in the Corinthian gift passage. "For by one Spirit we were all baptized into one body" (1 Cor. 12:13). Paul concluded this series of seven truths with a reference to God, whose oneness is the basis of the unity of His people. Paul had already made it clear that Christ had made it possible for both Jew and Gentile to have access in one Spirit to the Father (Eph. 2:13-18). Here Paul proclaimed that the one Father of all, who is over all and in all and through all is *Himself* the basis of the church's unity.

While Paul stressed that unity is a gift of God meditated through the Holy Spirit, he nevertheless impressed on his readers that it was also a goal toward which the church must strive. First, the phrase "being diligent to preserve the unity of the Spirit" reminded the readers that although they could not create unity, they must make every effort to preserve it. Second, like the call which must be lived up to, unity is such that it must be pursued through the edifying use of the gifts (4:12*b*-13). The final phrase of verse 3 "in the bond of peace" indicates that peace would be the end result of the living in love which preserved unity. In Colossians 3:14-15 Paul called love the perfect bond of unity. In the ministry passage of 1 Thessalonians 5:12 *ff.* Paul exhorted the Thessalonians to esteem the leaders in love that they may live in peace. Thus here, as in 1 Corinthians 12—14 and Romans 12, we discover the unique Pauline teaching: unity fostered by love is given practical expression in the body through the use of the gifts.

We must now look to the historical situation to gain some insight into this strong emphasis upon unity. In 1 Corinthians Paul stressed unity in order to combat the individualistic attitude of the spirituals, which manifested itself in the desire to exalt oneself and to choose one "spiritual" leader over another. In Ephesians the unity, which was fostered by the proper use of the gifts, was specifically related to doctrinal stability in the face of various heretical teachings. Notice in verse 13 that the goal of gifted ministry is unity of the faith. This then is immediately tied to the result: "We are no longer to be children, tossed here and there by waves, and carried about by every wind of doctrine" (v. 14). Thus the gift passage with its emphasis on unity and the practical explanation concerning its maintenance forms a vital part of Paul's positive protection from the heretical teachings threatening the churches of Asia Minor. Paul was aware that internal disunity left any church vulnerable to the "winds of doctrine." Notice that the familiar themes of spiritual gifts and unity of the body are again present, but they are specifically tailored to meet the needs of the churches being addressed.

It is important to point out that we are still dealing with an understanding of the church, the body of Christ, whose unity and peace is given by the Holy Spirit and maintained by the proper functioning of individually gifted members (4:11-16). There was no board of officials that could be called upon to restore unity. In the same light it is equally significant that Paul appealed to the proper functioning of all the gifted members—leaders and laypersons alike—rather than to a formal creed or church authority, as the primary protection against the cancerous spread of false teaching. We have not lost the vision of the fully-functioning gifted church in Ephesians.

This message of unity must be heard afresh in every generation. It is the only hope for churches and denominations alike. Diverse gifts and ministries should never be the cause of dissension. When properly appreciated and practiced they should lead to growth and stability. This will only be the case when they are properly understood as manifestations of grace, not signs of spiritual arrogance. Only then will they be properly employed for the good of the body of Christ. This appreciation for the diversity of gifts can help bridge many of the barriers that can separate us as fellow Christians.

Where is the Word *Charisma?*

Be prepared to discover some exciting new elements to add further to our understanding of the ministry of the gifted community. It is readily apparent to those who read the Greek that the term *charisma* does not occur in Ephesians 4. Although this might at first glance appear to be a rather significant matter, upon close examination it is found to be quite insignificant. *Charisma* was first used by Paul to refer to gifts for ministry in 1 Corinthians, where he used it to replace *pnuematika,* a term used by the spirituals to emphasize their advanced spirituality. Paul wanted to stress the graciousness *(charis)* of all manifestations of the Spirit to combat their arrogance and thus *charisma* became his word of choice. After writing 1 Corinthians, Paul used *charisma* in several contexts where it clearly bears a meaning less specialized than that of 1 Corinthians 12:4 (for example, 2 Cor. 1:11; Rom. 1:11; 5:15; 6:23; 11:29). Paul again used *charisma* in a specialized sense to mean "abilities for service" in the short passage on community ministry in Romans 12:6. Therefore, our translation of *charisma* is determined by its use in a particular context. It sometimes is used to refer to gifts for ministry and at other times it simply means free gift as in Romans 5:15 where it refers to the free gift of salvation. In the same manner we have seen in 1 Thessalonians that Paul could discuss community ministry without the use of the term *charisma.* Therefore it is the content of the passage which is important and not the presence or absence of a particular term.

Nevertheless, when we look at the terminology used in Ephesians 4:7-8, we discover similarity with earlier passages and an interesting modification, which can be understood in light of the historical situation posed above. You should recall that in both 1 Corinthians 1:4-7 and Romans 12:6, the introduction of *charisma,* in a specialized sense meaning "gifts for ministry," was clarified by its close relationship with *charis* (grace).

In Ephesians 4:7 the phrase: "But to each one of us grace was given" carried the same impact as "according to the grace given to us" in Romans 12:6. Each believer had been given an individualized expression of *charis* (grace), that is to say, an individualized empowering for ministry. Earlier in Ephesians 3:2 and 7 *ff.* Paul alluded to his empowering for ministry to the Gentiles by the use of *charis* and *dorea* (gift). Notice specifically 3:7: ". . . of which I was made a minister according to the gift *(dōrea)* of God's grace *(charis)* which was given to me according to the working of His power."

In Ephesians 4:7 Paul further explained that our individualized gift of *grace* was in accord with the "measure of Christ's gift." "Christ's gift" was immediately explained by the use of a quotation of Psalm 68:18, followed by Paul's comment on it. The phrase you should underline in the Psalm is "And He gave gifts to men." The word for gifts is *domata* and not *charismata,* but it means here the same thing that *charismata* does in 1 Corinthians 12:4 and other gift passages. Paul did not feel bound to use *charisma* to discuss spiritual gifts and thus he found *domata,* already present in the Psalm, as appropriate for expressing his message. The empowering for ministry *(charis)* and the corresponding visible expression of that empowering *(charismata/ domata)* are proclaimed to be the gifts of Christ to persons.

We need to notice that Paul didn't have such a hang-up with terminology as we do today. We hear someone use the words *charismatic church* or *Spirit filled* and we immediately draw lines that divide. How contrary this is to the Spirit and teaching of the New Testament. Every believer and every church is by nature charismatic in a true biblical sense. This does not mean necessarily that people speak in tongues or practice gifts of healing. It means they have experienced the grace of the Lord Jesus Christ in salvation and they possess God's individualized *grace* empowering them for ongoing ministry in the world today. Without this gracious empowering of God no ministry can be accomplished in any church.

For the charismatic reader, this should be a warning that to label a church as "non-Spirit-filled" or "non-charismatic" because that church does not speak in tongues is unbiblical and divisive. I have heard this implication stated in numerous ways. "Does your church have the Spirit?" "Why don't you attend a church where Christ is alive?" Any such implication ignores the clear teaching of Scripture and harms the body. The noncharismatic reader should be reminded that God's grace has endless unity and diversity and Christians are not called to stand in judgment over their brothers and sisters. The key questions concerning the proper use of spiritual gifts are "order and edification." This is more to the point than whether a certain gift is present or absent in a particular church.

I have no illusion that this book will change the vocabulary of the church concerning spiritual gifts. I too am caught in this dilemma. I am frequently asked if our church is charismatic. I feel I have to answer "yes and no" and then explain my answer based on how I understand the biblical teaching on *charisma.* Perhaps we can never escape this dilemma concerning terminology. Maybe this is simply another warning that we should avoid pigeon-holing one another by any label.

What is more essential is that we learn to appreciate the diversity of the family of God and follow closely the biblical directives for seeking and using God's wonderful gifts for ministry.

The Gifts of the Exalted Christ

The strong emphasis on the exalted Christ as the Giver of gifts is a unique and central element of this passage concerning gifts for ministry. Although Paul made it clear in 1 Corinthians 12:6,18, and 28 that God was the ultimate Source of the gifts, he gave particular attention in that passage to the ministry of the Holy Spirit in relation to the gifts. He particularly emphasized the *one Spirit's* ministry in creating unity, a unity fostered by the diversity of gifts which He distributes to each one individually as He wills. You will recall that we have already noted that the strong emphasis on the ministry of the Spirit in regard to gifts was caused in part by the Corinthians over-emphasis on spirituality. In Romans 12 where Paul wrote with no particular problem concerning gifts in mind, he made *no* explicit mention of the Spirit's role in dispersing the gifts. The stress was on God as the Author of the gifts (Rom. 12:3). In Ephesians 4, Paul did mention the Spirit's role in giving unity to the church, but clearly the emphasis of this passage is on the exalted Christ who gave gifts to persons.

Christ's authority as the Giver of the gifts was supported by a reference to Psalm 68:18. If you look up the Old Testament reference you will discover that the quotation here is not exact. The most important difference is the phrase "Thou hast received gifts among men" in Psalm 68:18 was changed to read "He gave gifts to men." This change is important since this established the point that Christ is the one who gave gifts to persons. It is possible that Paul simply paraphrased the Psalm adapting the reading to suit his purpose in this context. It is, however, interesting that the Targum on the Psalms (*Targum* denotes an Aramaic translation or paraphrase of some parts of the Old Testament) contains the same alteration from "receiving" to "giving." The Targum reads: "You ascended the firmament, prophet Moses, you took captivity captive. You learned the words of the law *you gave them* as gifts to the sons of man."[2]

We can't determine whether Paul himself under the inspiration of the Spirit paraphrased the Psalm or used a genuine pre-Christian Targum to Psalm 68:18, or knew of a Hebrew text which had "gave" for "received." Whatever the case, the triumphant ascent, the rule of Christ, and the giving of gifts to persons are the crucial elements Paul was stressing in the present context. This emphasis on the exaltation of Christ, His dominion over all powers, and consequently His filling of all things is consistent with the teaching of Colossians concerning the dominion of Christ. By applying this Psalm of Christ, Paul underlined the total sufficiency of the exalted Lord who Himself gives gifts to persons. This in turn strikes a telling blow against the heresy that would devalue Christ and thus His church. Because the church is the body of Christ, any attack upon the uniqueness or authority of Christ will, in the same instance, be an attack upon the church.

Verses 9-10 are a comment on "ascended" included to make it clear that it was the exalted Christ alone who was the Giver of gifts. The proper interpretation of these verses is a difficult matter. There is little agreement on how "lower parts of the earth" should be interpreted. Four main solutions have been offered. (1) The descent spoken of in the phrase "He also had descended into the lower parts of the earth" refers to Christ's descent into hell between His death and resurrection. It is often suggested that during this triumphant march through hell He released the captive souls. These are frequently interpreted to mean Old Testament saints who had believed in the hope of Messiah's coming. In the present letter, "He led captivity captive (KJV)" can best be understood as a reference, not to the release of captive souls, but to the victory over all spirits and powers (1:21) which previously ruled over humanity (Eph. 2:1-7 and Col. 2:15). This is a more natural understanding of the "captive" and thus rules against this first suggestion.

(2) Other scholars suggest that the descent here is after the ascent and therefore refers to the descent of the ascended Lord at Pentecost. There is no other New Testament reference in which Christ is explicit-

ly pictured as descending at Pentecost, with the exception of John 14:18. The Greek term here for descent is nowhere used for the descent of the Spirit at Pentecost. The interpretation of this passage in terms of the descent at Pentecost places primary emphasis on the *descent* whereas the clear emphasis of Paul is on the *ascension* of the resurrected Lord.

(3) A third view is that the descent refers to the incarnation of Christ. The "lower parts of the earth" simply describes the earth as the lower regions in contrast to the heavens above. This view has the advantage of being the most natural reading of the text. It is further supported by the fact that the same Greek word translated "descent" is used in John 6:33 and 38 to describe the descent at the incarnation.

(4) A final view is that the descent to the lower part of the earth refers simply to the physical death of our Lord and its significance for human redemption. It is important that this letter frequently underlines the saving significance of the death of Christ (1:20; 2:16; 5:2,25) which is linked with His resurrection.

It is difficult to decide between these final two options, and it is not particularly important to do so for our purposes since the main point in either case is made clear. Christ, who previously descended, has triumphed over all powers (including death) and has been highly exalted in virtue of which He fills all things. "For above all the heavens" has an impact similar to "for above all rule and authority and power and dominion" in Ephesians 1:21. This again reinforces the conclusion that "He led captive a host of captives" is a reference to Christ's dominion over all spirits and powers which previously ruled over humanity (1:21). It is the exalted triumphant Christ Himself who equips the church with gifted persons for ministry. This single truth, when fully accepted, should be sufficient to shake us from the lethargy of playing church.

We can again draw attention to the thematic unity of Ephesians and Colossians by looking at the similar idea expressed in Colossians 2:14 *ff.* Paul stated: "On the cross he discarded the cosmic powers and authorities like a garment; he made a public spectacle of them and led them as captives in his triumphal procession" (NEB). The triumph of Christ was in Colossians specifically related to the freedom of the believer (vv. 16-18) and to Christ's ability as the head of the body to supply all that is necessary for the growth of the church (v. 19). This emphasis on the relationship of the exalted Christ and the church is also found in Colossians 1:15-20. Yet the focus on the empowering of the church was a much more prominent theme in Ephesians. What Paul only mentioned in Colossians 2:19, he fully explained in Ephesians 4:7-16.

Therefore Ephesians 4:8-10 serves to clarify 4:7 by demonstrating the authority of the one who gave the gifts to the church. The content of this section is similar to that of Ephesians 1:20-23, where Paul stated that God has made Christ head over all things for the church. The believers were not members of an insignificant new sect, but a part of the universal church which was fully equipped by the Lord of the universe. Anyone tempted to believe that there were other avenues to divine fullness should realize that the fullness of the Godhead dwells in Christ and He alone fills heaven and earth. But beyond that the exciting news is that this fullness is experienced in the fellowship of the church which is His body. Paul's insistence that Christ is the Giver of the gifts can best be explained by understanding Ephesians as a positive and protective restatement of the theme of the exaltation of Christ in Colossians. Therefore this distinctive element of the Ephesian gift passage was related to Paul's purpose and point of view in the light of a unique historical situation.

I was standing in the driveway of a church I once pastored greeting the folks as they got out of their cars. As I opened the passenger-side door of the cars waiting to deposit their passengers under the covered driveway. I became intrigued by the animated conversation between a father and his son. The boy was obviously and uncomfortably dressed for church while the dad was dressed for golf or some other outdoor diversion. I surmised, quite accurately, that they were debating the value of church attendance. It was equally clear that the boy was losing. As I opened the door to the car I overheard the young boy's last attempt to convince his dad that he should be allowed to accompany him to the golf course.

"Dad, are you sure you attended church when you were a kid?"
Dad responded, "Yes Son I'm sure. Now go on."
The lad haughtily retorted, "Well I bet you it won't do me any good either."

When I tell that story from the pulpit, people usually laugh, until it dawns on them what is being implied. We attend church out of duty, go through the motions, but it really won't make any difference. Church membership and church attendance are frequently viewed as optional. We expect good fellowship and friendship, but really don't expect it to be a life-changing supernatural experience. If we ever come to grips with this truth that the exalted Lord fills the church with His fullness, that this is the place of full access to the resources of Almighty God, it will transform our churches and consequently our nation. I can never understand how someone can read what Paul said here and take church membership or attendance lightly. How can we be sporadic in our attendance at Sunday School or Sunday-night church? How can we view outreach as an option or watch as fellow members drop by the wayside? We are His body, "the fulness of Him who fills all in all" (Eph. 1:23).

Gifted Leaders to Equip Gifted Saints

Does this passage show a departure from Pauline teaching on the gifted community? There are some scholars who believe that the vision of a gifted community in which all members were gifted to share in the ministry has faded. They find here a stronger emphasis upon structure and hierarchy. I, however, believe that the thought of this passage is clearly consistent with earlier Pauline teaching. It does add a unique point of clarification concerning the relationship between gifted leader and gifted saint. The unique features can be explained by the demands of the new historical situation Paul was facing in Asia Minor.

Before looking specifically at the gifts mentioned in 4:11, there are several general issues which must be considered. In our study of 1 Corinthians we noticed Paul's insistence that the manifestations of the

Spirit were "given" and thus must be understood as the expressions of God's grace and not as spiritual privileges. This same emphasis was clearly seen in Romans 12:3 and 6. Is this theme also found in Ephesians? Observe that Paul used the verb *give* on three occasions (4:7,8,-11) and *gift* twice (4:7-8). The use of *charis* in Ephesians 4:7 likewise linked the empowering for ministry to the grace of God and thus ruled out all possibility of spiritual arrogance. Thus the theme of graciousness is equally present in Ephesians.

A majority of modern-day commentators would agree that one of the characteristic elements of Paul's teaching on gifts, was the insistence that *all* believers are gifted. This teaching is made explicit for the first time in 1 Corinthians, where Paul was combatting a narrow view held by some that only a few spiritually elite possessed the *pneumatika*. Paul insisted that each one had been given a manifestation of the Spirit, a point he vividly demonstrated by use of the body imagery. This same point is made in Romans 12, although in a less argumentative fashion, with the emphatic use of *each* in verse 3. Some commentators have objected that in Ephesians only certain individuals in leadership roles were pictured as gifted men. This is clearly not the case. The phrase "each one of us" in verse 7 leaves little doubt that every member had received *charis* according to the measure of Christ's gift. Yet, when the giving of gifts is specified in verse 11 we find a narrow list which included only persons who we might describe as leaders.

We are faced with an interesting question concerning the relationship of the leaders of verse 11 to the "saints" of verse 12. The debate at this point has often centered around the strength of the various prepositional phrases in this verse. Some commentators argue that all three phrases in this verse are coordinate and therefore conclude that the gifted leaders of verse 11 perfect the saints and do the work of ministry, thus edifying the body. If this view is taken, then we are dealing with a new concept of functioning within the church which placed virtually the total responsibility for ministry on church leaders. This idea would certainly be markedly different than the Pauline insistence that every member was a gifted minister.

On the other hand, other commentators argue that the two phrases "for the work of service, to the building up of the body of Christ" are subordinate to the phrase "for the equipping of the saints." In this case the gifted leaders were to equip the saints who do the work of ministry. This idea would be consistent with Pauline teaching. It would also constitute a more explicit elaboration of earlier teaching in that it would clarify the relationship between gifted leader and gifted saint.

It is difficult to make a decision about an interpretation when two commentators reach very different conclusions using the same prepositional phrases to support their own arguments. It is unlikely that any such decisions can be reached from the evidence of the prepositional phrases alone. Paul could have used different prepositions simply for the sake of variety. The weight of the evidence from other Pauline writings favors the interpretation that the leaders are to equip the saints so that the saints can do the work of ministry, but we must look at the present context for a final resolution of this question. It is important, therefore, that the section on gifts was prefaced by the insistence that each believer was given a measure of Christ's gifts. The conclusion of this passage is no less important. Notice that the growth of the body depend upon the proper working of "every joint" and "each individual part" (v. 16). It is from the head, Christ, that the body is empowered to grow. Yet growth comes only through the harmonious working of the individual parts. It is necessary for each member of the body to function in proportion to the gift with which the believer has been entrusted.

This teaching is consistent with that of 1 Corinthians 12:14 *ff.* and bears a striking resemblance to Romans where the phrase "according to the proportion of his faith" was used along with the body imagery to convey this idea. We can also draw attention to the general tenor of Ephesians. The emphasis throughout is on the riches received by *all* the saints through Christ. Nowhere was there the suggestion that some believers have special priority concerning the reception of any of Christ's benefits. The related concept that all believers belong to the body of Christ and therefore they must show mutual concern for one another is found throughout Ephesians (2:16, 4:25-29; 5:30), Ephesians 5:19 pictures an act of worship in which believers were encouraged to address one another in psalms, hymns, and spiritual songs.

We are justified therefore in concluding that the leaders were viewed as gifted members who had special gifts and responsibilities for enabling other gifted members to do the work of service, although this was not their only function. I conclude, therefore, that in terms of its teaching concerning the "given" nature of all abilities for service and the universality of gifts among believers, this passage is consistent with the whole of Pauline teaching. It does in fact enhance our understanding of the relationship between gifted members and gifted leaders.

I was once teaching a class on personal evangelism in a small church I served. I was full of excitement and anticipation. I was a new pastor, but I had been through this course in another church that I had attended while in college. I knew it would work, and I knew it was just what we needed. Attendance was excellent for the first few weeks and then it began to decline dramatically. I was frustrated and fell into the trap of preaching to the ones there about the lack of commitment of those who were missing.

A deacon raised his hand and quietly asked, "Preacher why are you teaching us about witnessing? We pay you to do that."

I was stunned! I couldn't believe what I was hearing. I felt like a hired gun. Preacher, you're the professional. You go get them! Often folks won't be as honest as this deacon was with me that night. Yet the feeling that the pastor is the only one gifted to minister is often prevalent in churches today. Someone's in the hospital—the preacher ought to go. I've got a friend who's unsaved—I had better get the preacher. We've got folks dropping out of church—the preacher doesn't visit. I'm not suggesting that the preacher shouldn't do all the above things. I am merely pointing out that every member is gifted for and responsible for ministry. One of the pastor's primary tasks is to equip the saints for the work of service. The pastor may discover someone in the congregation who has a beautiful gift for showing mercy. With encouragement and training this individual could become a priceless fellow laborer in the shut-in or hospital visitation ministry of the church.

The ministry of the New Testament church is a shared ministry in which the pastor helps the laypersons recognize, develop, and utilize their God-given talents for service. The biblical principle of "every-member-gifted" is one of the most affirming principles in the Word of God. You are gifted and you should be ministering in your church family.

The Gift List

We must now consider the actual listing of gifts here in Ephesians 4. From our study of earlier passages we have come to expect a gift list when we discuss spiritual gifts. Yet there are scholars who have found this particular list troublesome because the gifts here are persons and because these persons appear to be officials of the church. We must, therefore, look at these objections.

In this context there is a twofold emphasis: gifts are given to persons (4:7-8) and gifted persons are given to the church (4:11). Despite the objections of many writers, this is not an emphasis which is unique to Ephesians. Look at 1 Corinthians 12:28 and you find a particularly close parallel to this passage. "And God has appointed in the church, first apostles, second prophets, third teachers." In 1 Corinthians Paul not only spoke of the gift of prophecy, but of a prophet who had been appointed to the church. In the gift list in Romans 12:6-8 Paul moves quite freely from abilities to persons. Thus the fact that gifts mentioned here are gifted persons should not surprise us. It simply illustrates the close relationship between the individual and the gift one possessed. For example, we can refer to an individual as a teacher or as a person who has a gift for teaching. In either case we understand what is being communicated.

Yet we cannot ignore the fact that all the gifts mentioned here are specifically related to leadership functions. That does make this list distinctive. Why then do we have only leadership gifts mentioned?

The answer is to be found by attention to the specific historical context.

Let's review for a moment our finding concerning the earlier gift lists. I suggested that the first gift list found in 1 Corinthians 12:8-10 included only the "extraordinary" or "ecstatic" gifts which were eagerly sought by the "spirituals." In the second list (1 Cor. 12:28) Paul placed apostles, prophets, and teachers first in the list to demonstrate that church leaders were also gifted for ministry. Secondly he introduced two "service" or rather "mundane" gifts, "helps and administrations," to broaden even more the Corinthian understanding of manifestations of the Spirit. In the Romans 12:6 gift list Paul did not mention the ecstatic gifts such as healing or tongues, but he placed his emphasis on service gifts and leadership gifts.

This tendency to emphasize leadership, teaching, and service gifts is again quite clear in Ephesians 4. The importance of the service gifts is clearly emphasized by the underlining of the ability of all members to contribute to the body's growth. The leaders serve to equip the saints for their work of service ministry. The body depends on the "proper working of each individual part," (v. 16) whether gifted leader or gifted member.

The actual gift list was restricted to leadership-teaching gifts because of the particular historical situation being addressed. Paul placed apostles, prophets, and other teachers at the center of this passage to counteract the heretical teachings present in procounsular Asia. While Paul never intended that any gift list would be comprehensive, that did not mean that the particular gifts mentioned were not intentionally selected.

In each case the selection of gifts to be included in a particular gift list was determined by the unique needs of that particular historical situation. The common element shared by each gifted person listed in Ephesians 4:11 was their function in teaching or preaching the gospel. The whole impetus for the writing of Colossians and Ephesians was the heretical doctrines with which these churches were faced. In Colossians Paul emphasized the importance of the apostolic tradition of teaching (1:5 *ff.*,23; 2:6 *ff.)* and its expression through the ministries of men such as Epaphras (1:7 *ff.* and 4:12 *ff.*), Tychius (4:7 *ff.*), Onesimus (4:9), and Archippus (4:17). It was therefore appropriate that Paul's discussion of the proper use of gifts in this Ephesians passage focused on unity of faith and stability in the face of the false winds of doctrine and the schemings of men. It is equally understandable that Paul would emphasize the gifted leaders who were responsible for teaching and proclamation functions in the church.

When we give full weight to the historical situation, the appropriateness of placing the apostles and prophets at the forefront of the gift list is quite understandable. Yet two earlier references to apostles and prophets in Ephesians 2:20 and 3:5 have prompted some writers to argue that in Ephesians both the prophets and apostles are viewed as a past institution. But upon closer examination we will notice that both passages contain an implicit allusion to the teaching function. The apostles and prophets in 2:20 are foundational because they received, believed, and gave witness to the message on which the church should be built. Paul's specific concern in 3:5 was to underline the validity of his own message that the church was made up of Jews and Gentiles alike. This message, once hidden, had now been revealed through the holy apostles and prophets. Both of these passages serve to underscore the authenticity of the church and its teaching. This emphasis can best be appreciated if we understand that Paul was fighting against heretical teachings.

This has been a passage that has always given me the greatest encouragement about my active involvement in the local church. We all encounter people who see their church membership as a matter of convenience. It appears to be little more than another entry on their resumé. It is placed on a par with belonging to a civic club. Correspondingly attendance is sporadic and service and stewardship are nonexistent.

When we begin to understand the full weight of this letter, such a lackadaisical attitude is utterly unthinkable. Through our relationship with Jesus Christ, we have been joined to His very body. We give visible expression to this decision by publicly professing Him and thus uniting with a local church. Our connection with this local body of believers unites us with the eternal work of God. We are given opportunity to build upon a foundation established in the apostles and prophets, one which has Jesus Christ as its cornerstone. It has been empowered by the resurrection and ascension of our Lord. Listen to this truth in the words of Paul: "He put all things in subjection under His feet and gave Him as Lord over all things to the church which is His body, the fullness of Him who fills all in all" (Eph. 1:22-23). How can we be apathetic or causal when we have been granted such a priviledged opportunity? We might ask one further telling question: Why are many churches so impotent when God has empowered them and gifted them with His fullness?

Before we finish considering this gift list, we should point out yet another unique feature. The listing of evangelist and pastor are new to the Pauline lists. We have noticed that "new" gifts have been found in every list subsequent to the first one in 1 Corinthians 12:8-10. I would further suggest that if Paul were to have addressed this matter several more times, he would have perhaps added others as the situation required. Those who attempt to number the Pauline gifts and then group all the various ministries of the church around certain divisions of gifts misunderstand the dynamic nature of Paul's teaching. God uniquely gifts His church for each new task and ministry as the need arises. There is nothing static about God's ability to empower His church for each new challenge. Certainly many of the New Testament gifts remain operative as the *need continues*. Gifts, such as teaching, administration, and showing mercy, to name a few, will always be needed by the church. Yet with the advent of technological advances, many churches require persons with technical skills and gifts in electronics or sound engineering to help facilitate their ministry. We should not apologize for thinking of these abilities for service —when rightly understood as a gracious gift of God and surrendered to His service through His body—as spiritual gifts.

Evidence suggests that we are more conscious of "titles" and "offices" than were the Christians of the first century. The terms here are descriptions of functions and this explains, in part, the difficulty in coming to a conclusion as to whether the phrase "pastors and teachers" refers to one ministry or two. Because they are both governed by one article in the Greek, it is possible that Paul was describing two functions of a single individual. It is interesting that the functions of shepherding and teaching are similar to those mentioned in 1 Thessalonians 5:12. Whether the two functions of teaching and shepherding would have been exercised by one individual or several could have depended upon the local situation, the size of the Christian community and the gifted persons available to the church.

The Interlocking of Pastor and Layperson

All too often I sense in many churches a "we" versus "them" spirit concerning the pastor and his staff. Some pastors almost unconsciously talk about their church members in terms of *"those folks* who don't have any vision." I hear pastors lament, "I just can't get *these folks* to do anything." Did you hear the subtle division that occurs with the mention of "these folks." It is as if the pastor is saying, "I'm not a part of them." On the other hand I hear church members talk about their pastor or staff as virtual outsiders. "We've got to be careful! The pastor is always trying to get *us* to spend *our* money." The pastor is an outside influence trying to get *us* to change. We'll never become what God intends us to be as a church until we drop these artificial barriers. We are one body of gifted folks with interrelated gifts and responsibilities. This close linking of pastor and gifted saints is most clearly described here in Ephesians.

Here we find a coherent and detailed discussion of the working together of all community members—those with leadership abilities and those with service abilities. The principle that gifted members are to assist one another is certainly not a new one (see 1 Cor. 12:7,25; 14:3,31; Rom. 12:5 *ff.*). The teaching that among the gifted members there are some who possess leadership and teaching gifts and responsibilities is also not new. The body imagery in 1 Corinthians and Romans both imply that mutual cooperation is essential to proper growth. In 1 Thessalonians 5:12 *ff.* without any allusion to *charismata,* Paul urged respect for the leaders and encouraged all the members to minister to one another. Yet it is here in the Ephesian Letter that this principle was fully clarified.

One of the ministries of those who were gifted to serve in leadership roles was the "equipping" or "furnishing" of the saints for a full use of their gifts in service to the community. Don't be put off by the use of the word "saint." Be assured that Paul is talking to you. Every Christian is addressed as a "holy one," or one called out for service to God. You might find it interesting to inform your spouse that you now understand that you are a "saint." See what reaction you get! More seriously, notice that Paul saw no apparent conflict in the suggestion that a person was gifted by God for service and yet still needed the pastor to equip him or her for the work of service. The verb that Paul used here contained both the concepts of "preparing" and "making complete." To say that a person is gifted, does not suggest that they do not need further teaching and training in order to fully utilize their God-given gifts.

We recognize this principle when we encourage a young person who feels called to the pastoral ministry to go to seminary to complete their training. Yet we must further understand the practical ramification of this biblical teaching in the life of the local church. Because we find a person who is gifted to teach doesn't mean that we should arm them with a quarterly and thrust them headlong into a room of fifth graders. They do need and deserve to be further equipped. They not only need to "complete" or sharpen their God-given skills, they need theological instruction and information concerning the full responsibilities of service. This is a priority calling of every pastor and every church. The church is indeed empowered to serve by the gifts of the Spirit, but it is prepared for effective service through the equipping ministry of training. Divine empowering and human cooperation go hand in hand.

The Results of Gifted Ministry

The phrase "to the building up of the body of Christ" expressed a goal which, in Ephesians, was viewed in both a short-range and long-range context. Let's review for a moment the emphasis on edification in earlier gift passages. The goal of edification received its fullest expression in the Corinthian correspondence, where Paul found it necessary to combat a desire to use spiritual gifts for the sole purpose of exalting the possessor. In chapter 14 Paul exhorted the Corinthians to seek gifts with the greatest potential for edification, and to utilize any gifts already possessed in a manner which would edify the brethren. The goal of edification was not as explicit in Romans 12 but was nonetheless present (see vv. 5 and 9 *ff.*).

It is not surprising, therefore, to discover that the theme of "edification" or "building up" of the body occurred twice in the Ephesian gift passage. In Ephesians 4:13 the theme of edification through the proper use of gifts was developed in two positive directions, both of which were consistent with Paul's concern in the entire letter. Paul desired for them unity of the faith and a full measure of spiritual maturity. These two phrases further define the building up of the body. In verse 14 the results of the proper use of gifts was applied specifically to the dangers of false doctrine which threatened these communities. Edification which resulted in unity and maturity would enable them to stand against the pressures of false doctrine.

The phrases "unity of the faith" and "knowledge of the Son of God" are bound together both by the Greek construction and also by the context of the sentence. The themes of unity and knowledge received special attention in both Colossians and Ephesians because of the unsettling heretical influences present in procounsular Asia. It is often difficult to determine whether the word *faith* refers to the idea of believing in Christ unto salvation or the objective content of that belief (doctrine). The emphasis on knowledge and the mention of false teaching indicate that faith here must be given an objective content. Personal belief in Christ committed a person to the objective truths which they had been taught (Col. 2:6-7 and Eph. 4:20-21). Knowledge of this body of truth which they had been taught in Christ (4:21) would give these early Christians stability against false teaching. Sound doctrine is still the church's mainline defense against heretical influences.

We can gain a fuller understanding of Paul's desire that they grow in the "knowledge of the Son of God" by a quick review of this letter. In Ephesians 1:15 *ff.* Paul told them that he had not ceased to pray that they would receive "a spirit of wisdom and of the revelation in the knowledge of Him" (v. 17). This "knowledge of Him" was further defined as an understanding of the hope to which they have been called, the riches of His glorious inheritance in the saints, and the immeasurable greatness of His power which is available to the believer. Thus the reference to "the knowledge of the Son of God" in 4:13, contained both the idea of the personal relationship with Christ and a full understanding of the riches that are available to the believer in Christ Jesus. Paul wanted to show these churches how utterly futile it was to search for any spiritual blessing outside of Christ. Why would one do so when Christ is the fullness of Him who fills all in all? This same theme was explicitly stated in Colossians 2:2ff.

It is easier to point out the mistakes of earlier generations than it is to learn from them. Why do many of our own young people look for spiritual meaning and fullness in cults or psychic phenomena? Is it possible that they have seen little evidence of God's fullness in the life of their church? Could it be that we have not taught them to experience the fullness of blessings available to them in Christ? There are other threats to the church which are more subtle. The suggestion that something or some experience must be added to the Christian life in order to receive the fullness of power and blessing is also dangerous. We frequently hear the teaching that one must receive a second act of grace, or the baptism of the Spirit subsequent to salvation to know the fullness of God. Paul's emphasis in this letter and others was that the fullness of the Godhead was available in Christ alone. The believer must come to a fuller knowledge of the Son of God and thus fully open himself to the total blessing already available to us in Him. We must continually and habitually be seeking this flow of God's power through us. The suggestion that salvation requires any other act or event to complete it is to slide toward a dangerous and nonbiblical emphasis.

The phrase "unity of the faith, and of the knowledge of the Son of God" stressed both the *unity* of Christian belief, in contrast to the diverse winds of doctrine, and the full *sufficiency* of Christ, in the face of every claim to provide wisdom or spiritual power through another means. Paul made this positive and bold assertion to combat the childish behavior of those who were being blown off course by every wind of doctrine. If they sought the fullness of Christ, they would discover the abundance for every good work. They needed to grow in knowledge, not seek another spiritual experience. Yet the tendency remains. It is much easier and more emotionally gratifying to seek subsequent mystical or spiritual experiences than it is to discipline oneself to grow in the knowledge of God.

The ultimate goal of the full utilization of gifts was growth to maturity which is measured by the fullness of Christ (v. 13). The meaning of the phrase "fullness of Christ" is difficult to interpret, but is nonetheless important to our understanding of this passage. This phrase picks up the tension of the "already" and the "not yet" which governs this entire passage. Simply put, the "already-not yet" is the tension of becoming what one already is in Christ. Remember that this section began with the demand that the Christian live in a manner worthy of the calling with which he had been called. In Ephesians 4:3, unity was said to be a gift of the Spirit ("already"), but in verse 13 it is a goal ("not yet") to be sought through the proper use of gifts. Knowledge also was a promised possession that Paul desired that these Christians would come to fully possess (Eph. 1:17-18; 3:18-19). Thus knowledge is at once a gift to be received ("already") and a goal to be reached ("not yet").

For a more complete understanding of this important principle let's review earlier references in this letter "to the fullness of Christ." In Ephesians 1:20 *ff.* Paul declared that Christ was the fullness of God, who fills all in all. Specifically he noted that God had placed everything in subjection under Christ's feet for the advantage of the church. In Ephesians 3:14-21 Paul prayed that the readers would personally experience this fullness of God in terms of inner strengthening, the indwelling presence of Christ, and an overflowing abundance of love. Notice too that this power that works through us will glorify Christ in the church (3:20-21). In Ephesians 4:10 *ff.* Paul clarified the way in which this fullness of God was experienced in the church. Christ has ascended and descended that He Himself might personally fill all things. He does so through the distribution of gifted persons to the church. The "fullness of Christ" therefore refers to the completeness which is already realized by the body of believers in Christ, but which must be attained in every respect. It is at one time a "gift" and a "goal," a "blessing" and a "calling."

"Fullness of Christ" then serves as a focal point for this passage. Christ, who fills all things, fills the church and thus empowers it to become what it is called to be. This phrase thus gathers up all the elements of growth expressed in phrases such as unity of the faith, knowledge of the Son of God, and maturity. Now we must draw attention to the fact that this process of growth in all things is accomplished through the full and proper utilization of the *gifts,* as each member works according to his own measure. It is through the service of the gifted members that the divine energy flows. Paul was challenging those who might be tempted to seek spiritual fullness elsewhere, to take advantage of the full resources of God already available to them in Christ.

As you can see, much is at stake in the proper understanding of spiritual gifts. Both the reading of this book and the study of the gift passages cannot be simply academic exercises. While you may have begun this study out of curiosity to find out what would be said about "tongues" or some other specific gift, it is my prayer that your interest has gone much deeper. It must be the hunger of every pastor and every layperson to grow in this full knowledge of the Son of God. We must allow the divine power to flow through us and thus through our churches by the proper working of a gifted membership.

In verse 14 these goals and potentialities are brought into focus by a sharp contrast with the current historical situation. To be blown about by every wind of doctrine was indeed childish when one realized that the church has the sufficiency of the fullness of Christ. The phrase "every wind of doctrine" probably bore testimony to the pluralistic religious atmosphere in proconsular Asia which Paul was offering protection against. It may also denote the transitory value of these teachings compared to the truth revealed in Christ. These winds will soon pass! The contrast between the mature person of verse 13, and the children of verse 14 could not be more striking. Paul often used *children* to imply a certain childish instability which could lead to disunity and the enslavement to fleshly desires (see 1 Cor. 3:1; Gal. 4:3). Here the children were described as those who were unstable and who therefore might prove to be easy prey for deceitful persons. Those who would seek after deeper wisdom through sources outside Christ were fittingly compared to a small rudderless boat which was tossed about freely by the action of the mind and the waves. Paul's evaluation of the false teaching is obvious. They were simply the deceptions of crafty men, and their attractiveness lay only in the ability of the deceitful teachers to make them so.

Paul was not reprimanding the Christians for behaving like children, but warning them of the dangers of false teaching. Paul intentionally painted the picture in a stark black and white so that he might prevent these Christians from succumbing to human trickery and schemes.

The Proper Working of Each Individual Part

Paul concluded this section with a positive but general emphasis on the responsibility of each member for the growth of the church until the ultimate goal of maturity was reached. That goal was defined simply as growing in "all aspects into Him who is the head, even Christ." Therefore the gifts will be fully and necessarily operative until the return of the Lord. This reminds us of the emphasis of 1 Corinthians 13.

The phrase "speaking the truth in love" provided a pungent contrast with the scheming of the false teachers (v. 14). The emphasis on spoken truth was necessary to curb the dangerous winds of doctrine swirling throughout proconsular Asia. The speaking of the truth must occur in the context of love. It is significant that this passage begins and ends with the phrase "in love." In no other New Testament writing does this formula occur as often as it does in Ephesians (six times). "In love" describes the sphere of the Christian life and the manner in which all Christian ministry is to take place. The gifted body not only grows toward unity and maturity, but it does so in the ethical context of love.

Speaking the truth in love presents a twofold contrast with the false teachers of verse 14. The false teachers were presenting *false* doctrine in a *deceptive* manner, the church grows through the proclamation of the *truth* in *love*. This phrase also links this section with the ethical teaching which follows in verse 17 and beyond. Growing into the fullness of Christ therefore not only means growth in unity and doctrinal stability, but it involves ethical maturity as well.

The ultimate goal of Christian growth was repeated in verse 16 but with new terminology designed to emphasize the present process of growth. Paul here gave the reader a close look at the inner workings of the community which was in the process of growth. Therefore this section serves as something of a summary, Paul brought together four prominent themes of this passage and related each of them to the present work of the church in its pilgrimage to become what it has been empowered to be in Christ.

(1) The church is enabled to grow because Christ, the Lord of the universe, fills it. The reference to Christ as the head in verse 15 was intended to direct the reader's attention to the practical ramifications of being the body of Christ, who is Lord of the universe. The energy *(energeia)* for growth comes from God through Christ (see 1:11,19; 3:7,20). Thus it is Christ Himself who empowers the body to edify itself in love. This should put an end to the two most popular words in the church today: "We can't." Our source of empowering should rule out timidity when we are called to ministry.

(2) Although the empowering for growth comes from God through Christ, the body members themselves are fully involved in the growth process. The divine energy is channeled "by that which every joint supplies." Some commentators object to Paul's medical picture since the joint itself has no power. That objection misses the point entirely. The joint is like a fulcrum through which the empowering of God is magnified and applied in the realm of this present age. I will never forget when my dad demonstrated the application of power through

a fulcrum. We needed to remove a large rock from our garden. After watching me struggle to remove the stone by direct force, he directed me to find a small log for a lever and a larger log for a fulcrum. The obstacle was easily removed as the lever and fulcrum channeled and magnified my energy. Our gifts become the channel for the focusing of divine power in the life of the church. In the Christian community every individual must fully utilize his or her own gift for the growth of the body. It is through the proper utilization of the gifts of every member that divine fullness will be experienced. This emphasis was echoed in the final phrase in which Paul stated that divine power working through every member enabled the body to build itself up in love.

(3) The unity of the Spirit was necessary to bring diversely gifted members into a harmoniously working body. The emphasis on *every, each,* and *proper working* stressed the demand for unity and mutual support in the utilization of spiritual gifts. Notice once again that gifts make us dependent on one another. One body member working alone can accomplish little and soon becomes spiritually impoverished due to a lack of personal edification from other body members. At the same moment, the body is hurt because of the failure of a necessary body part to function properly.

(4) The full utilization of spiritual gifts and the resulting growth must take place in the context of love. Thus the spiritually gifted community is not only distinguished by its full possession of gifts through which divine energy flows, but it is also marked by its divine nature. If we recall the argument of 1 Corinthians 13, we should note that even the fullest expression of gifts had no spiritual value where love was lacking. For example, we might find a person who is a skillful teacher but who does not teach in a spirit of love. No edification would occur and thus this would not be a proper working of a gifted body member. As a result there will be no growth of the body.

Having examined the content of this passage concerning such matters as the source, nature, purpose, and results of the gifts, I maintain that Ephesians 4:1-16 can be placed quite comfortably in the developing continuum of Pauline thought concerning the ministering community. Although its content is consistent with earlier teaching, ideas only implicitly contained in other passages are pressed forward, and new elaborations are discovered. I suggest that the peculiar emphasis of this passage can be understood if we accept the suggestion that Paul wrote this letter to guard against the spread of the dangers mentioned in Colossians.

Conclusions

I have suggested that Ephesians was written by Paul as a positive deterrent against the heretical influences present in proconsular Asia. These influences are more clearly seen in the companion letter, Colossians. Ephesians was a circular letter which was delivered along an early Christian mail route composed of the seven churches mentioned in Revelation. The letter was first delivered to Ephesus by Tychicus. From there it was passed along by messenger to Laodicea, from where it would be shared with the Colossians. More tentatively, I suggested that Colossians, although written specifically for the Colossian community, was probably shared with this same wider audience.

The teaching of Ephesians and Colossians is therefore complementary. It is particularly important to underline the stress on the dominion and authority of Christ in both letters. In the Ephesian letter this emphasis was specifically related to the ministry of the church. Notice that any attack upon Christ would necessarily have the effect of challenging the claim of the church to be His body—empowered by Him. From our vantage point we must notice that unless we have a proper view of the full impact of Christ's divinity, our churches will be powerless.

The absence of the term *charisma* causes no problem in our understanding of this "gift passage." The term *charis* (grace) functions as it does in Romans 12:3 and 6 and refers therefore to the individualized empowering for ministry. Paul actually replaced *charismata* with *domata* because of the quotation of Psalm 68:18 in Ephesians 4:8. Again we notice that Paul was more concerned with developing an understanding of the empowering for ministry than with the significance of a particular word.

This passage is similar to Romans 12 in that its tone is nonpolemical. This suggests that Paul was not aware of a specific abuse of misunderstanding related to the "gifts" in proconsular Asia. Both can be contrasted with Corinthians where confusion and abuse prompted a detailed treatment of gifts. Therefore it is essential that we keep in mind all of these passages when we formulate our own understanding of spiritual gifts. It is worthy of note that Ephesians 4 shows more clearly than does Romans 12 the impact of a specific historical need. Here the concern was over the spread of heretical teaching.

It becomes clear that when this passage is interpreted in light of its historical context, its teaching can be placed comfortably within the continuum of Paul's thought.

(1) In a manner consistent with 1 Corinthians 13 and Romans 12 Paul again drew attention to the broader context of the ethical aspects of Christian existence. Gifts must be utilized in the context of love which empowers them to edify the brethren. This is accomplished by placing this entire passage in the context of ethical teaching and by the repetition of the phrase "in love" (4:2,5,16).

(2) This passage again underlined Paul's assertion that *all believers* were gifted and that the growth and edification of the body can take place only when all the members function according to their own charismatic potential ("in measure").

(3) There was again an emphasis on the "graciousness" of all capacities for service.

(4) Consistent with the lists of 1 Corinthians 12:28 *ff.* and Romans 12, Paul emphasized leadership and service abilities. Here the more "spectacular gifts" were not mentioned. Their value was more for the individual than the assembly.

(5) The church was again viewed as the body of Christ for whom unity is both a "gift" and a "goal." The unity of the Spirit was to be maintained and striven for by the proper functioning of differently gifted members.

In spite of the fact that this passage has much in common with earlier passages, it adds several unique new emphases to our under-standing of gifts. Like Romans, Ephesians does not specifically con-nect the giving of gifts with the ministry of the Spirit. I think Paul avoided this connection to short-circuit any spiritual arrogance like that in Corinth. We would do well to heed this note today. In Ephe-sians, the gifts were said to be given by the ascended and exalted Lord who thus empowered His body for ministry and growth. Paul's desire to counter, in a positive measure, the heretical tendencies present in proconsular Asia, accounts for this distinctive emphasis on the exalt-ed and sufficient Christ.

The listing of gifts in Ephesians is unique because it included only persons who might be thought of as "leaders." Notice that this list does closely parallel the first half of 1 Corinthians 12:28. In Ephesians the stress on leadership and teaching gifts were more pronounced because of Paul's desire to ensure doctrinal stability.

Here, for the first time, there is a clear statement concerning the relationship between those gifted for leadership and other gifted mem-bers of the community. The leaders must promote the ministry of the saints and equip them so that *all* may work together for the edification of the body.

The theme of unity was stressed as strongly here as in 1 Corin-thians, yet with a different application. In 1 Corinthians, Paul was combatting an egocentric spirituality which threatened the unity of the church from within. Here Paul was primarily concerned with stabilizing and enhancing internal unity in order to combat external pressures created by false teachers. Thus we have the unique emphasis that gifts properly used would lead to doctrinal stability and protect the believers from the winds of false doctrine which threaten the church.

As eschatological tension which was clearly evident in 1 Corin-thians 13 and 14 is also present in Ephesians 4, but is applied quite differently. In 1 Corinthians, Paul found it necessary to demonstrate that "gifts" did not have value as a "sign" that one already "reigns" in a sense implied by an "overrealized" eschatology. The gifts were evidence that one lives in the *now* (present age of the church) and must be used accordingly. In Ephesians, Paul's intent was only positive. He demonstrated that the gifts were supplied by the exalted Lord Himself and as such fully equipped the church to become what she was intended to be as the fullness of Christ. The church was empowered to become in unity, knowledge, and ethical maturity what she already potentially was in Christ. Ephesians challenges us to unleash through the church the mighty power of the ascended Lord.

The body imagery in Ephesians at first appears to be different. Christ is called the head of the church which is His body. This is not to be taken in a biological sense as if He were one among many of the members. The emphasis on "headship" simply picked up the theme of the Lordship of Christ. He is head over the church by virtue of which He fully equips her for ministry.

Paul again made it clear that every member can and must contribute to the upbuilding of the body by ministering according to his or her own gifts. The situation in Ephesus demanded a strong emphasis on leadership gifts because of the heretical influences. This does not suggest that the church in Ephesians had a more structured leadership than other churches such as those in Thessalonica, Corinth, or Rome. We have noted throughout this study that, for Paul, a charismatic community did not mean a community without clearly recognizable and responsible leadership. May we all, leader and gifted member alike, be called back to the divine principle of every-member ministry. May we allow the full power of the resurrected and ascended Lord to *empower the church today!*

Notes

1. W.M. Ramsay, *The Letters to the Seven Churches.* (London: Hodder and Stoughton, 1909), p. 171 *ff.*

2. Cited from M. McNamara, *The New Testament and the Palestinian Targum to the Pentateuch* (Rome: Pontifical Biblical Institute, 1966), n. p. n.

8
Pulling It All Together

I hope that we have together developed an appreciation for the depth of Paul's teaching concerning spiritual gifts. As with any biblical topic, we have only touched the surface of a profound subject. My greatest desire is that you have learned some truths which have challenged you to grow spiritually. When the church lays hold of the power available through the risen Lord we will begin to experience the renewing transformation we so desperately long for. We will see dormant churches burst forth into new life and God's people march forth throughout this land in a mighty army. May we once again hear folks say: "Those Christians, they're turning the world upside down."

It is unnecessary to repeat the conclusions which have been set out at the end of each chapter. However, in a book of this length, it will be helpful to draw together in a comprehensive fashion some of the conclusions and implications of this study.

A Low-Altitude Overview

I have a friend in Tidewater Virginia who frequently takes me flying in his six-seater airplane. I enjoy the advantage of being able to fly at altitudes much lower than the airlines are permitted to fly. The experience of flying over the same area at varying altitudes has taught me to observe how different features of the landscape stand out at different altitudes. For example, looking down on Tidewater from an airliner at thirty-thousand feet one can see the different creeks, rivers, and bays of Tidewater. From this vantage point they look like so many crooked fingers grasping at each green, wooded area. From this high vantage point you can see the pattern develop as small branches become larger rivers as they join forces in a march to the bay.

At a lower level, from windows of the plane, details of those waterways come out of hiding. The deep channels stand out as dark-colored ribbons against the expansive regions of shallow waters. The convergence of river with river is marked by a murky battle. If we descend even lower, we begin to notice that the waterways are teeming with life. There are huge naval vessels, barges, fishing boats, and small speedboats full of teenagers. The waterways from this altitude are alive with activity. We could have only guessed about these details from thirty-thousand feet.

If we continue this analogy of travel, our study has placed us on the ground in each of our communities, walking the streets with Paul. We've attempted to come to grips with the unique historical events which shaped each community and consequently Paul's letter to that community. We've picked up every little clue and paid attention to the detail. Perhaps now it would be worth our while to board our six-seater plane together and fly back over the whole of our trip at a relatively low altitude focusing on the prominent features of each community.

Before we taxi out for takeoff we would do well to recall that we have detected a certain progress in Paul's thought concerning the ministry of the community. We found in 1 Thessalonians 5:12-22 several ideas in seminal form which would become central to Paul's teaching on the gifted community in 1 Corinthians 12—14. For example, we discovered an emphasis on the responsibility of all believers to minister for the common good of the community. Paul underlined the necessity of respecting those who provided for the community leadership and teaching. When all work together out of mutual concern for the brethren, unity and peace will be the end result.

Yet, in 1 Thessalonians there was no hint that all believers were "gifted" and consequently no discussion of the source, nature, or purpose of gifts. There was no listing of gifts and no body imagery to demonstrate the unity which emerges from diversity.

The difficulties of the Corinthian community, where some individuals were boldly displaying their miraculous gifts, provided both the catalyst, and in some respects, the shaping force for the development of Paul's thought concerning the functioning of the charismatic community. In reaction to an aberrant and narrow view of the "manifestation of the Spirit," Paul for the first time insisted that all believers were gifted. He further declared that the manifestations of the Spirit were better understood as manifestations of God's graciousness. He pointed out that there were a variety of gifts for service and those included leadership, teaching, and service abilities. It is this variety that enables the church to function properly. Thus we can see that the gifts were not given to create spiritual pride, but for the edification of the church. It is in 1 Corinthians 12—14 that we have the *first,* the most *extensive* and the most *situationally determined* passage concerning Paul's teaching on *charismata.*

Several elements of Paul's teaching, hammered out in reaction to the abberant thinking of the spirituals in Corinth, were then synthesized in a clear and nonpolemic fashion in Romans 12. Again in Ephesians 4 Paul developed the central ideas of 1 Corinthians 12—14 in a more general fashion. Here, however, they were taken a step further and reapplied in order to meet the challenges offered by the heretical teaching now emerging in proconsular Asia. It can be seen therefore that the natural progression in Paul's thought was occasioned by the challenges presented by each new historical situation. The Holy Spirit thus moved Paul to elaborate and reapply concepts which are clearly discernable throughout his teaching.

Thessalonica

With this instrument check of reminder completed, I think we will find it helpful to take our small plane back over each of our communities in turn and isolate in brief fashion the unique features which appear from this quick low-level pass. While 1 Thessalonians 5 does not contain the term *charisma* the ministry of the community is nonetheless addressed. The concepts of ministry discussed in this letter were specifically related to the needs of this community. Paul was particularly concerned to uphold the true leaders in Thessalonica to ensure for continued growth and stability in his absence. Paul not only exhorted the brethren to respect and esteem those over them in the Lord, but he warned them that despising prophetic proclamation was tantamount to quenching the Spirit. Paul further appealed to all believers to be about the work of ministry. Notice that Paul listed specific tasks which were of immediate concern to this local congregation.

Corinth Revisited

In 1 Corinthians the term *charisma* appeared for the first time. Its selection and use must be understood in light of the historical situation. The spirituals *(pneumatikoi)* of Corinth referred to their miraculous abilities as *(pneumatika)* "Spiritual manifestations" because they believed the miraculous gifts were a sign that they already reigned (overrealized eschatology). In an attempt to counter this misunderstanding, to stop the immature boasting of the spirituals, and to bring harmony to the community, Paul declared that "manifestation[s] of the Spirit" were actually experiences of God's graciousness *(charismata)*. A proper understanding of grace would eliminate all boasting and spiritual elitism.

To counter the childish spiritual arrogance of Corinth, Paul made it quite clear that the Spirit was at work in *all* believers enabling them to confess Jesus as Lord and incorporating them into the one body. He contended that each believer had been given a manifestation of the Spirit for the common good and that therefore the unity of the body depended on the proper functioning of all members. The use of the body imagery to picture the working of the Christian community occurred for the first time in Pauline writings in 1 Corinthians. This common imagery of the body provided for Paul the perfect tool to illustrate that all body members are mutually interdependent, and all are gifted for unique functions in the community. Yet Paul took the imagery one step further to establish forcefully that those body members which might, from a human standpoint, appear to be less significant, were in fact to be given greater honor.

This point was clearly applied as Paul broadened the accepted understanding of "manifestation of the Spirit" by including in 1 Corinthians 12:28 gifts of leadership, teaching, and service. This gift list was the casting of the die. From this point on Paul would stress the greater value of intelligible gifts in the community because they were better suited for the edification of the body. Notice for example that in chapter 14 Paul contrasted prophecy and glossolalla. Paul's preference for prophecy was based on the fact that it was intelligible to both believers and nonbelievers. The discussion of prophecy and glossolalia has implications for all gifts. Paul used these two highly valued gifts in Corinth to demonstrate the priority of the "greater gifts." Greater gifts refers to those gifts most suitable for the edification of the body.

First Corinthians 13 was an original composition of Paul and it was the very apex of his argument against the spirituals. He demonstrated that "gifts" do not prove one to be a spiritual person. Love alone stands as a clear indicator that one is a spiritual person. The description of love in verse 4-7 was placed against the picture of the spirituals which had emerged in the first 12 chapters of 1 Corinthians. Thus in chapter 13 Paul established the basis upon which he could urge those who were truly spiritual to desire the more edifying gifts. It also enabled him to establish the pattern for the use of gifts already possessed and the control of all gifts. Love is evidenced in the life of the community in terms of edification. In the final verses of that chapter Paul demonstrated that gifts are intended for the church in the present age and therefore have meaning in the "now" as they are used in the good of the body.

Chapter 14 is nothing more than the practical outworking of making love one's aim. In the context of one's desire to edify the body, the spiritual gifts should be earnestly sought. They enable persons to express love in the life of the community. Paul left little doubt that the spiritual person would seek the gift of prophecy, one of the intelligible gifts, because the whole church would be edified and the nonbeliever would be made aware of God's presence. The gift of tongues uninterpreted left the nonbeliever and the Christian, without that gift, unedified. When interpreted, tongues could be of value for the church. Nevertheless, it must be remembered that tongues may still be offensive to the nonbeliever. Therefore Paul instructed the tongues speaker to avoid this danger by giving the interpretation only. This would require no audible use of tongues and thus avoid the risk of offending the unbeliever.

Specific regulations for controlling the gifts are found only in 1 Corinthians 14 and these too are best understood in light of the Corinthian difficulties. Paul's desire was to establish order on a broad basis which would be acceptable to all. He appealed to the nature of God, who is not a God of confusion. Therefore all gifts that truly express God's nature, when used properly, would not lead to confusion. The spiritual person can and must control personal gifts out of consideration for edification. Nevertheless, Paul did establish certain external regulations which were designed to silence those who were not concerned for the edification of the body.

Rome

Romans 12 is a more neutral passage than 1 Corinthians 12—14. Hence the insistence on sober evaluation, edifying use of the gifts and the listing of only leadership, teaching, and service gifts can best be explained in the light of Paul's recent confrontations with the Corinthian spirituals. Paul believed that the central concepts concerning the ministry of all believers were of value for other communities, but he wanted to guard against an arrogant and exaggerated understanding of gifts such as had developed in Corinth. Because of the nonpolemic nature of Romans 12, several points stand out clearly above the general landscape. Paul indicated that the individual who was being transformed by the renewing of the mind could and must properly discern his or her charismatic potential and fully employ the gift for the good of the whole. The absence of "miraculous" gifts and the very general nature of some of the gifts listed, such as "showing mercy" and "giving," along with the leadership and teaching gifts, make it abundantly clear that Paul wanted to exalt those gifts which were most suited to the edification of the body.

Proconsular Asia

The unique emphases found in Ephesians are to be accounted for by Paul's desire to protect the churches of proconsular Asia from heretical teachings. These false teachings are clearly reflected in Colossians. Accordingly, Paul declared that the church was equipped by the exalted Christ, the Lord of the universe, who gives gifts to persons and in turn gifted persons to the Church. Paul emphasized leadership and teaching gifts because of his desire to establish the authority of the individual leaders of these churches and to ensure doctrinal stability. The theme of unity, which is found in all the passages concerning gifts, was here uniquely applied to the concern for protection against heresy.

A Synthesis of Pauline Gift Theology

If we set aside for the moment the emphases and applications which are particularly related to a unique historical situation we may synthesize Paul's gift teaching as follows. (1) Every Christian is empowered by the Spirit to confess "Jesus as Lord" and in thus incorporated into the body of Christ expressed through fellowship in a local community of believers. (2) Every member of the community is gifted for service and thus can and must work for the good of the body. (3) The gifts are the consequence of God's graciousness. They say nothing about the level of one's spirituality, but everything about God's goodness to equip His body for service. (4) Every believer has a unique function in the body, therefore all are necessary and all depend upon the ministry of others. It is therefore essential that believers care for one another. (5) All community life must take place "in love," including the desire for and use of the gifts. (6) Gifts have as their single aim the edification of the body. (7) The gifted leaders must be recognized, esteemed, and obeyed so that all may function in peace. They are called to equip other gifted members to properly utilize their gifts in order that all together may build up the body in every aspect unto Christ.

A Higher Vantage Point

Perhaps we should now take our plane up a few thousand feet and from this vantage point draw together in a systematic and topical fashion conclusions which have been reached on certain issues of interest concerning the *spiritual gifts.*

A Comment on Terminology.

It appears that often today Christians are divided by the use of certain words. "Are you charismatic?" What does the questioner mean? Perhaps we should take a lesson from Paul. I have suggested that *charisma* is not a technical term and that it therefore takes on a special significance only when the context makes it clear that such is the case. A general meaning such as "favor," "benefit," or "gift" is necessary in 2 Corinthians 1:11; Romans 1:11; 5:15; 6:23; 11:29; and possibly in 1 Corinthians 7:7. In Ephesians 4:8 *charismata* was replaced by *domata* because of the use of the Psalm. Yet the context in Ephesians leaves little doubt concerning the topic of discussion, and therefore the omission in Ephesians 4 underlines the fact that it is the *concept* and not the *term* which was important to Paul. The term *charismata* was most important in 1 Corinthians where it was intentionally contrasted with *pneumatika* to establish the gracious nature of gifts. We should thus be careful of using terms such as *charismatic* or *Spirit filled* to label fellow believers. We need to deal with content and meaning when we discuss "gifts of ministry."

The Enmeshing of Gifts and Ethics

The interlocking of these two ideas was detected in 1 Thessalonians 5:15. However, the situation in Corinth, where manifestations of the Spirit were ascribed tremendous value but where immorality and self-seeking reigned, elicited a detailed description of the spiritual person (ch. 13). This chapter was central to Paul's argument and formed the basis for the practical discussion of gifts (ch. 14). Paul made the ethical context even more apparent in Romans 12 and

Ephesians 4 by literally surrounding the discussion of gifts with ethical teaching.

This insight suggests something about the relationship between the fruit of the Spirit and the gifts of the Spirit. The fruit of the Spirit is related to what an individual is and the gifts are related to what he or she does. The fruit of the Spirit enables the differently gifted members to forebear one another in love. Therefore it is the proper context of all genuine charismatic activity. The gifts in turn provide the means for the believer to express love in the context of the community in terms of edification. Both the fruit and the gifts are equally necessary for the ongoing life of the Christian community.

The Nature of the Charismata

Are *charismata* merely heightened natural abilities? Are they supernatural abilities given at salvation which have little, if anything, in common with natural abilities. Some have gone so far as to suggest that gifts are "activities of the moment." Let's first make a few observations. Paul included as gifts abilities, old and new, miraculous and seemingly mundane, momentary and permanent. They can be sought, controlled, and developed. The believer can be encouraged to seek certain gifts such as those that more easily edify. They can be controlled in the sense that the tongues speaker who cannot interpret can refrain from speaking, or the prophet who is interrupted can be silent. They can be developed through the ministry of the pastor-teacher who is to equip saints for the work of the ministry. When Paul spoke of *charismata* he was referring to "abilities" and "functions" which enabled an individual to minister to the body of Christ. Any attempt to number the gifts is to miss the spontaneity with which Paul listed the gifts. Our sovereign Lord is able to equip the church for any task it faces. Therefore He is able to create and empower new gifts for ministry as new challenges emerge.

I would suggest that there are three elements which must be present in an authentic spiritual gift. First it must be discerned to be the gracious gift of God, not an achievement of human will or an accident of birth. For the Christian there is no *natural* ability. The believer can now clearly see that all abilities for service are the manifestation of God's grace. Second, having discerned this truth, the believer is led to surrender his or her gifts in ministry to the Lord in the context of His body the church. At this point the desire is often born to develop these gifts through training or equipping. Thus we would encourage a young pastoral candidate to go to seminary or a Sunday School teacher to attend training seminars. It poses no conflict to speak of a spiritual gift and the need for equipping. Finally, they will be used selflessly in service to others for the edification of the body. When these criteria are met there is a unique and special outpouring of God's Spirit which empowers the individual for service. All of us have experienced the awareness that the results of our teaching, preaching, singing, and so forth was more than the simple addition of perspiration, preparation, and presentation. We are then humbled to recognize the Spirit's empowering working through our gifts.

Perhaps you are somewhat disappointed that after all this study we have not been able to give a simple definition of spiritual gifts. Believe me I have struggled with this dilemma for many hours. Perhaps this points to the mystery and awesomeness of our God who supplies our every need. Rather than attempt to tie down a workable definition, perhaps we should give greater effort to discovering and fully utilizing the multiplicity of gifts that are available for the church on mission.

It is helpful to pose a few questions to cause us to think more specifically on this matter. Most Christians that I have talked to have not given testimony to receiving new abilities for service at the point of their conversion. I have, however, been involved in the discipling process when an individual made the discovery that all ability comes from God (1 Cor. 4:7). This knowledge has led to believer to a humble commitment to use personal abilities in service to the Lord in the fellowship of the church. Perhaps I can illustrate this in the area of administration.

As our church has grown the administrative task has become increasingly more complex. It has been my pleasure to see men and women in our congregation discover that their skill with numbers and administrative details could be used for the Lord. One particular accountant in our church became immersed in the process of securing a building loan for our church. While this began for him as an extension of his business skills, it culminated in the awesome awareness that God had taken this surrendered ability and enabled him to serve through it beyond his human capacity. It was exciting to hear him say to the Church Council, "I prepared the materials, but what happened in that conference room was not my doing. It was beyond my ability." Is this a legitimate uncovering of a spiritual gift already possessed?

Paul taught that the believer could seek the higher gifts and that the leaders were to equip the saints for their work of ministry. This suggests that the church can help people discover and employ new gifts. The young pastor in the growing church is bombarded by the demands to administrate. He laments that his gift is preaching and caring for people. Yet he sees that to be effective at accomplishing these goals, he must fulfill some administrative duties. He prays, he reads, he seeks help from various resources and he develops his gift to administrate. It may in fact become his greatest ministry skill. Is this the discovery of a new gift graciously given by God who has promised to supply our every need? Thus it seems apparent that our sense of calling to a specific task or ministry provides the best clue for the discovery and development of our spiritual gift. God would not lead us to an area of ministry where He will not empower us for effective service.

Gifts Function in the Body

The very nature of gifts means that we are all interdependent. No matter how gifted a person may be, he has no life or ministry without the proper working of all other gifts. This should put a halt to all the arrogant and false spirituality which leads anyone to think he or she is too big for the church. "I just can't find a church good enough" rings with the spiritual arrogance of the Corinthians. "I don't need the church to be a Christian" rings with the foolishness of a mere infant who has not come to grips with his own dependent nature. This should make us value our membership and fellowship in the local body of believers where we are enriched and ministered to by the multiplicity of gifts possessed.

Further, we can suggest that even the most abundantly possessed gift has no meaning when taken out of the context of the church. Let me illustrate by looking at the gift of evangelism. Let's suppose that we have two evangelists who appear from all obvious criteria to be equally gifted. One evangelist comes to town on his own, rents the local arena, puts out posters, and draws a great crowd. You watch as people stream the aisles nightly. Six months later you meet with the local pastors' association and inquire, "Did any of you see any visible results from the crusade in your church?" After much discussion it is determined that local churches were not edified, nor were new Christians added to the body of Christ. On the other hand, an evangelist comes to the community with the stipulation that the local churches must be in agreement with his coming. Counselors are trained and those who respond to the invitation are encouraged to unite with a local church. All the follow-up is focused on the nurturing of the new Christians in the life of local churches. Which evangelist exercised properly the spiritual gift of evangelism? Any ability exercised for personal attention, without due concern for the body of Christ, is not properly used.

Paul spoke clearly to this issue in 1 Corinthians 13:2 where he pictured one possessing the gift of prophecy to the highest degree who did not exercise the gift in love. He was therefore found to be "nothing." A gift exercised outside the context of love is a bothersome noise and renders the person useless and personally unfulfilled. For example the gift of administration can degenerate into a numbers consciousness that ceases to truly care for the people behind the numbers. I have seen this happen when zealous Sunday School teachers insist that inactive members be dropped from their rolls because they are hurting the class's average attendance. Love demands that those statistics and numbers be translated into people who must be reached through the fellowship and ministry of the class.

We should note that the body is rendered less effective when any member doesn't serve according to the measure of his gift. No one is unimportant in God's economy. Yet the body is bigger than the mere compilation of its component parts. Ministry can continue, even if it occurs at a less-than-optimum efficiency. God can graciously graft in new parts to replace those parts which remove themselves from the life of the body. Conversely, however, a body part devoid of the body has no life nor empowering for ministry. A hand, even a very skilled one, once separated from the body loses its usefulness. This should stand as a warning to all those who think they can exercise their gifts with no connection or accountability to the church which is the body of Christ. Apart from the body there is no empowering and consequently no fruitfulness.

The history of the church is pockmarked with individuals who were once gifted and mightly used of God, who are now but empty shells with limited usefulness. Sometimes they separated themselves from the body out of arrogance and self-directed ego. Others separated themselves more subtly because they failed to function in the context of humble, loving service to the brotherhood. Others ignored the ethical context of the community and compromised their distinctive. Whatever the cause, the loss of empowering is apparent. A non-Christian observer might look on a once-powerful preacher and conclude that nothing has changed. His delivery may still be powerful, his illustrations crisp, and his content good. Yet the results are clearly lacking. Why? A spiritual gift is empowered by the Spirit of God only when recognized as a gracious gift, committed in service to the Lord, and humbly exercised in loving service to the body. When these criteria are lacking, the external appearance may be the same, but the loss of empowering will be evident.

The control of charismatic activity is a matter of live interest. There are those who argue that it should not and cannot be controlled. "I can't contain myself." "You would be quenching the Spirit if you prohibit me from speaking." Those statements simply do not square with the evidence of Scripture. Here 1 Corinthians is important, but it must be understood in light of its historical situation. The specific rules were laid down to prohibit those from speaking who would use the platform to demonstrate their gifts without any concern for the good of the body. The whole of chapter 14 was aimed at establishing internal and volitional controls. The authentically spiritual person would exercise restraint so as not to cause confusion. Gifts are related to the human will in such a way that the more edifying gifts can be sought and all gifts can be controlled and employed in an orderly manner. If the volitional control is ignored, external control can be invoked. Paul's regulations are an example of external control. In Ephesians 4:12 as well as 1 Corinthians 12:28 and other passages there is the clear teaching that God Himself has ordained a certain structure within the church and therefore Paul anticipated that the leaders should exercise some control over gifted ministry.

The Importance of Tongues at Corinth

A specific discussion of a single gift—like tongues—would be outside the scope of this present book. Nevertheless our overview prompts the question as to why tongues were so prominent in the Corinthian correspondence and yet did not occur in any other community ministry passage. We noted that they were eagerly sought in Corinth because they were thought to provide *audible* and *verifiable* proof that an individual already reigned, that is that he or she was a spiritual person. It is likely that they actually thought tongues were the language of the angels. We have no evidence that this theological idea had spread outside the Corinthian community. As to how tongues came to be so highly valued in Corinth one can only speculate. The suggestion that Paul encouraged enthusiastic manifestations in the worship of any community which he founded is clearly doubtful. There is an awkward silence concerning the ecstatic element of the spiritual life in Pauline writings, other than in 1 Corinthians. In that letter he treated it with considerable restraint. Tongues could have been introduced by another teacher who visited Corinth, such as Apollos, but we could only guess. It is possible that the desire for tongues was a very natural desire to repeat what God gave as a sign gift to numerous individuals as recorded in Acts. All of us have been guilty of trying to recreate the mood of a profound religious experience. Any attempt to force ecstasy of any sort will ultimately lead to excess.

Taking the full scope of Paul's teaching, it is apparent that Paul placed a heavy premium on the less spectacular gifts because they were better suited for the edification of the body. This is not to say that Paul disparaged tongues or the ecstatic element of the religious experience. You will recall that he gave testimony to his own experience of tongues. Paul viewed ecstatic experiences as a very personal occurrence which were of value to the individual, but not for the church as a whole. Paul concluded that his visionary experience was so profound that it could not be communicated. His considered opinion was that when he was outside himself in the grip of religious ecstasy it was for the Lord, but when he was in control of himself it was for the church.

A Final Thought

You may not agree with all the findings or conclusions of this book. We rarely find any book we agree with fully. But we can all agree that God has given to the church both a great calling and an abundant empowering for service. We have been accorded the highest honor when He called us "His body." In Ephesians 1:22-23 Paul related the glorious resurrection and exaltation of Christ to the church with these words:

> And He put all things in subjection under His feet, and gave Him as head over all things to the church, which is His body, the fullness of Him who fills all in all.

How can we ever play at church when such great power has been given to us? How can we be satisfied to go through empty motions with a lost world at stake? How can we continue to let petty jealousies and squabbles disrupt the unity required for effective service? We must become what we are called to be! We must utilize the full empowering of God! We must claim and utilize the gifts at our disposal! We must move as a mighty army empowered by the Spirit of God.

My heart's desire for the church can best be expressed by bringing together two central elements in Paul's teaching: "Make love your aim, and earnestly desire the spiritual gifts, . . . strive to excel in building up the church" (1 Cor. 14:1a,12b, RSV). *Amen.*